Tinou Le Joly Sénoville

Sweet Treats
in cross-stitch
53 delightful projects to embroider

Photography by Frédéric Lucano
Styling by Sonia Lucano

MURDOCH BOOKS

Wall hanging
instructions page 64
chart page 107

Contents

Projects 5

Wall hanging 2
Tablecloth and napkins 6
The three gourmands 8
Labels 10
Bed tidy 12
Small toy 13
Pennant 14
Notebook 15
Small bags 16
Box 17
Baby pants 18
Baby bottle cover 19
Apron 20
Heat-mat 21
Three cushions 22
Macaron bag 24
Cloth case 25
Tea cosy 26
Placemat 27
Chef's toque 28
'Watch out for moustaches!' napkin 29
'Too good' napkin 30
'Absolutely chocolate!' napkin 31
Tote bag 32
Badges 33
Little girl dress 34
Headscarf 35
Bunting 36
Big bag 37
Bib 38
Medium bag 39
Eclair tea towel 40
Chair cover 41
Letter and number games 42
Equation cushion 43
Pocket tidy 44
Jar 45
Announcement card 46
Lolly bags 47
Recipe book 48
Apple pie wall hanging 50
Apple tea towel 51
Gift ribbon 52
Gift tags 53
Handkerchief 54
Small shoulder bag 55
Singlet 56
Small tags 57
Birthday cards 58
T-shirt 59
Placemat 60
Napkin 61
'C'est chic' wall hanging 143

Instructions 63

Charts 83

Projects

Tablecloth and napkins

instructions page 64
chart pages 86–87

"mes petits gateaux"
LE VRAI! Petit OURSON
GUIMAUVE FANTAISIE ENROBÉE DE CHOCOLAT AU LAIT
FANCY MARSH MALLOW COATED WITH MILK CHOCOLATE

The three gourmands

instructions page 64
charts pages 88–93

Labels

instructions page 65
charts pages 88–93

NON CONSIGNE

FRESH
NEW
COOL,DRAY
AIRTIGHT,
PROOF
FRESH
strawberry
good
1 2 3
9 4 5 6
Cueillir des Cerises

Bed tidy

instructions page 65
charts pages 94–95

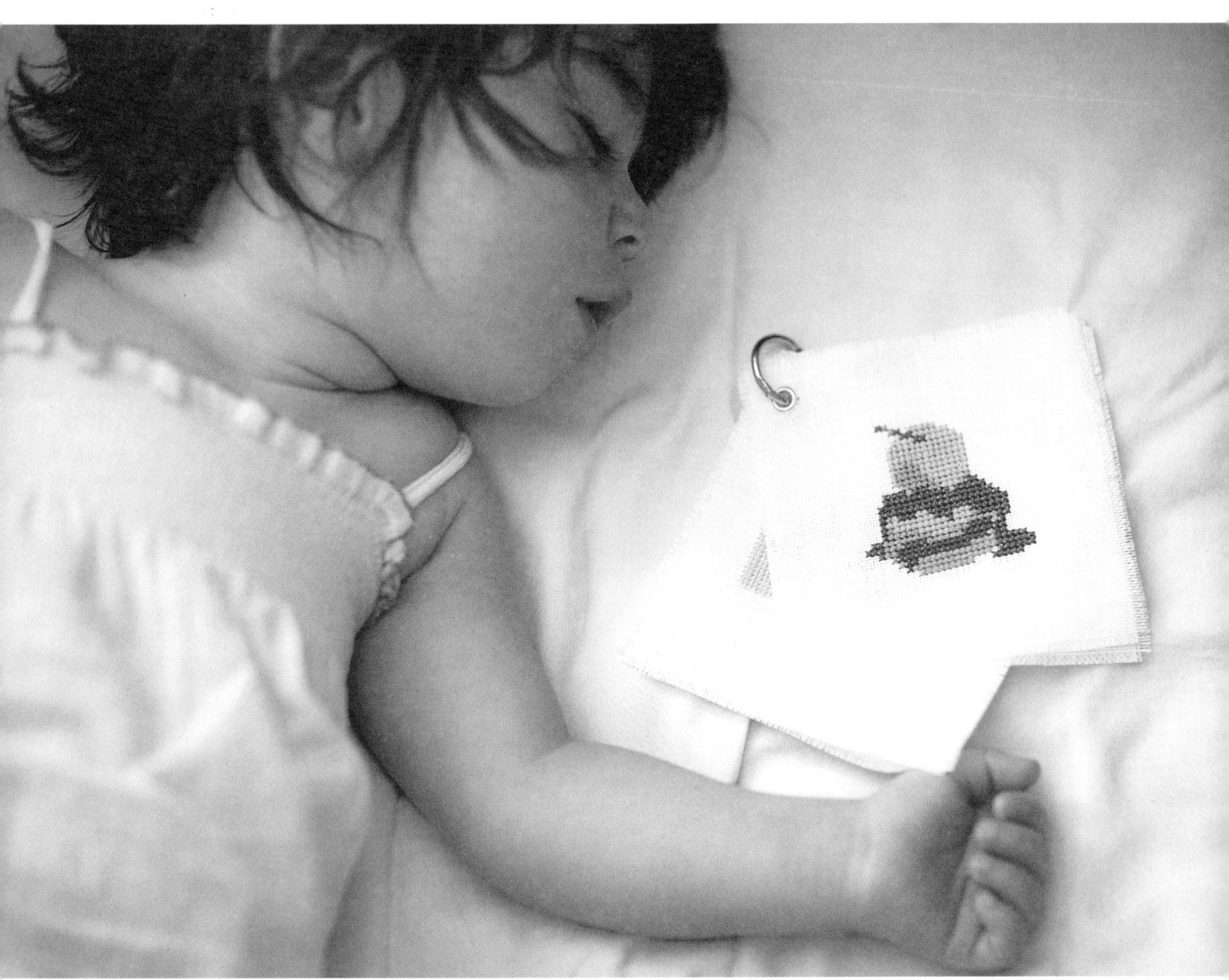

Small toy

instructions page 65
charts pages 94–95

Notebook
instructions page 66
chart pages 96–97

Pennant
instructions page 66
chart pages 96–97

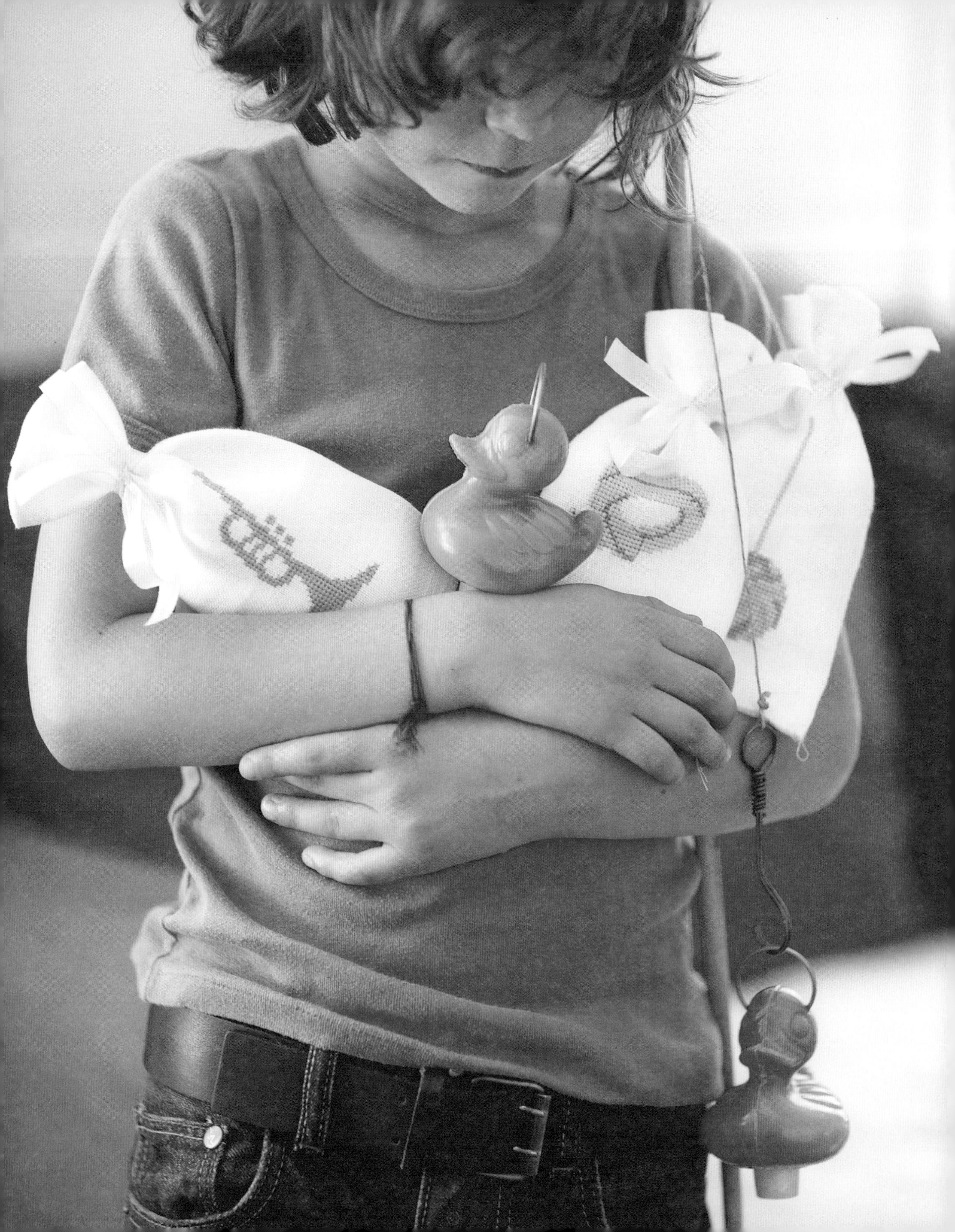

Small bags

instructions page 66
charts pages 99 and 100–101

Box

instructions page 67
chart pages 96–97

Baby pants

instructions page 67
chart pages 100–101

Baby bottle cover

instructions page 67
chart pages 100–101

Crêpes
œufs

Apron

instructions page 68
chart pages 102–103

Heat-mat

instructions page 68
chart pages 102–103

Three cushions

instructions page 69
chart pages 104–105

Macaron bag

instructions page 69
chart pages 106–107

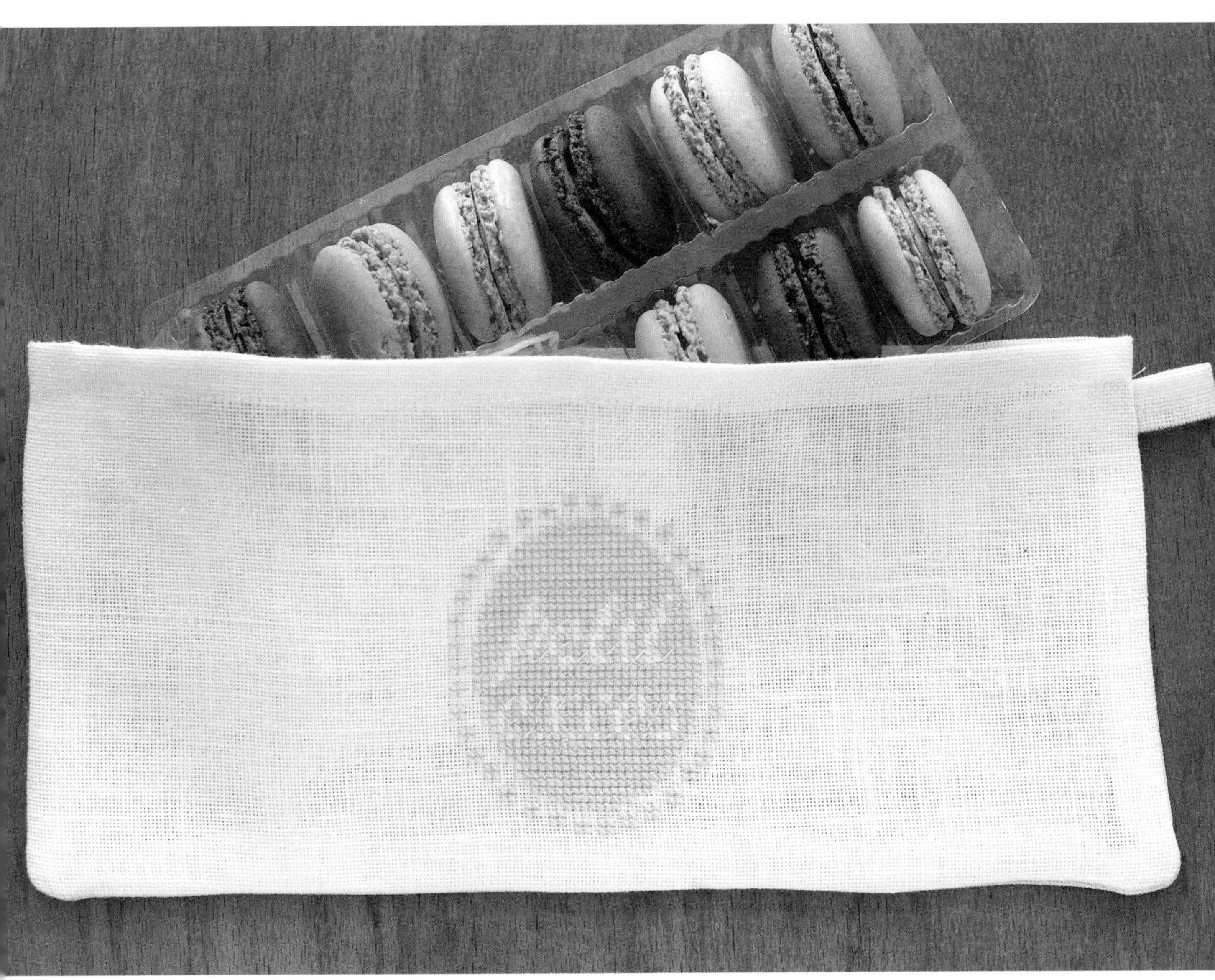

Cloth case

instructions page 69
chart pages 106–107

Tea cosy

instructions page 70
chart pages 108–109

Placemat

instructions page 70
chart pages 108–109

Chef's toque

instructions page 70
chart pages 110–111

'Attention aux moustaches' ('Watch out for moustaches!') napkin

instructions page 71
chart page 139

piece of cake
ece of cake

'Trop bon!' ('Too good!') napkin

instructions page 71
chart pages 104–105

'Carrément chocolat!' ('Absolutely chocolate!') napkin

instructions page 71
chart pages 110–111

Badges

instructions page 72
charts pages 112–113 and 134

Tote bag

instructions page 72
chart pages 112–113

Headscarf

instructions page 73
chart pages 126–127

Little girl dress

instructions page 72
chart pages 114–115

Big bag

instructions page 73
chart pages 116–117

Bunting

instructions page 73
chart pages 116–117

JOURS
de
fete

Bib

instructions page 74
chart pages 118–119

Medium bag

instructions page 74
chart pages 118–119

Eclair tea towel

instructions page 74
chart pages 120–121

Chair cover

instructions page 75
chart pages 120–121

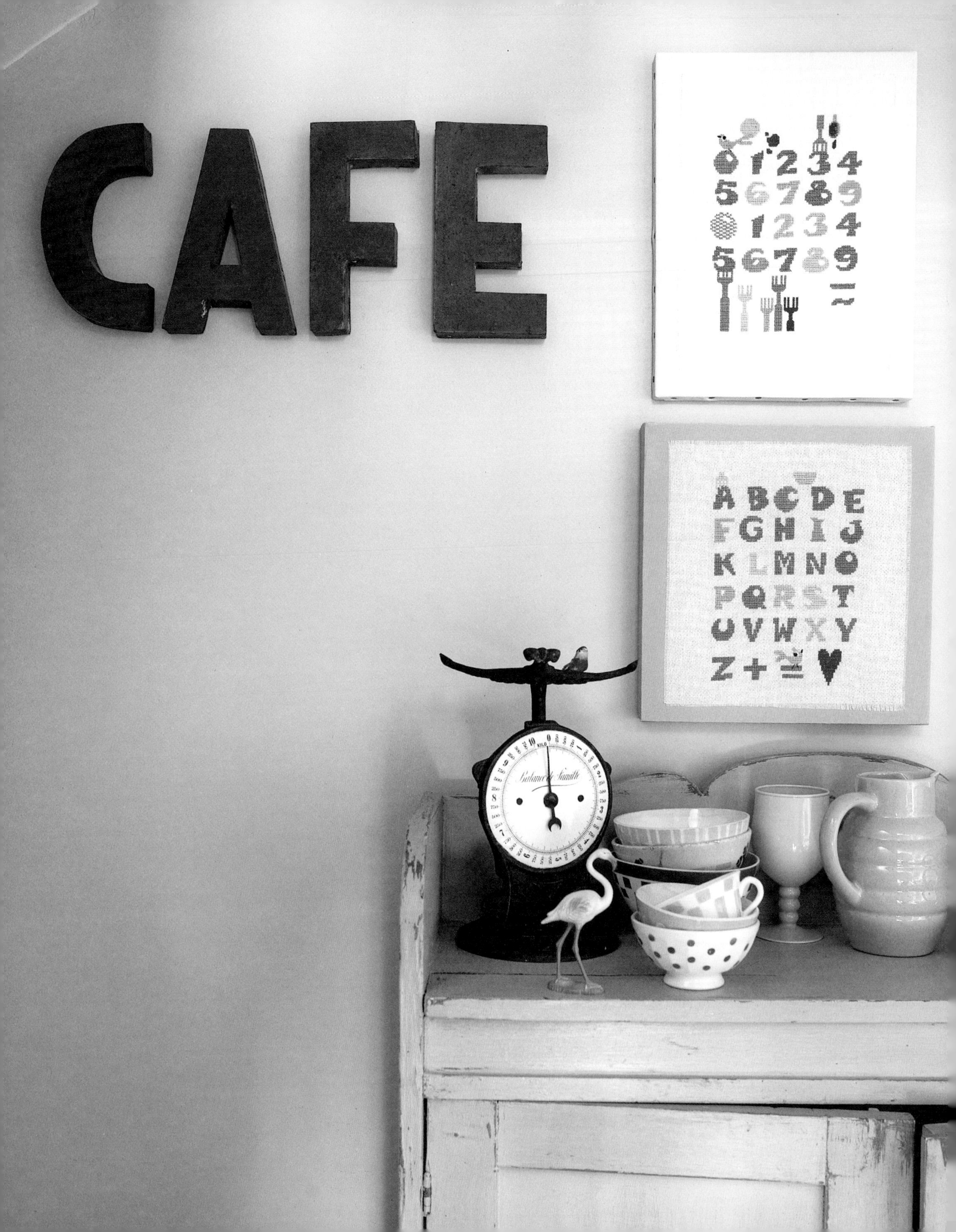
CAFE
ABCDE
FGHIJ
KLMNO
PQRST
UVWXY
Z + =

Letter and number games

instructions page 75
chart pages 122–123

Equation cushion

instructions page 75
chart pages 122–123

herbes
herbs
erbe
ma

Pocket tidy

instructions page 76
chart pages 124–125

Jar

instructions page 76
chart pages 124–125

(9Juillet 2009)
la
LUMIERE

Announcement card

instructions page 76
chart pages 126–127

Lolly bags

instructions page 77
chart pages 126–127

Recipe book

instructions page 77
chart pages 114–115

très frais !!!

Apple tea towel

instructions page 77
chart pages 128–12

Apple pie wall hanging

instructions page 77
chart pages 128–129

Gift ribbon

instructions page 78
chart pages 130–131

Gift tags

instructions page 78
chart pages 130–131

Handkerchief

instructions page 78
chart pages 100–101

Small shoulder bag

instructions page 79
chart pages 132–133

Small tags

instructions page 79
chart page 135

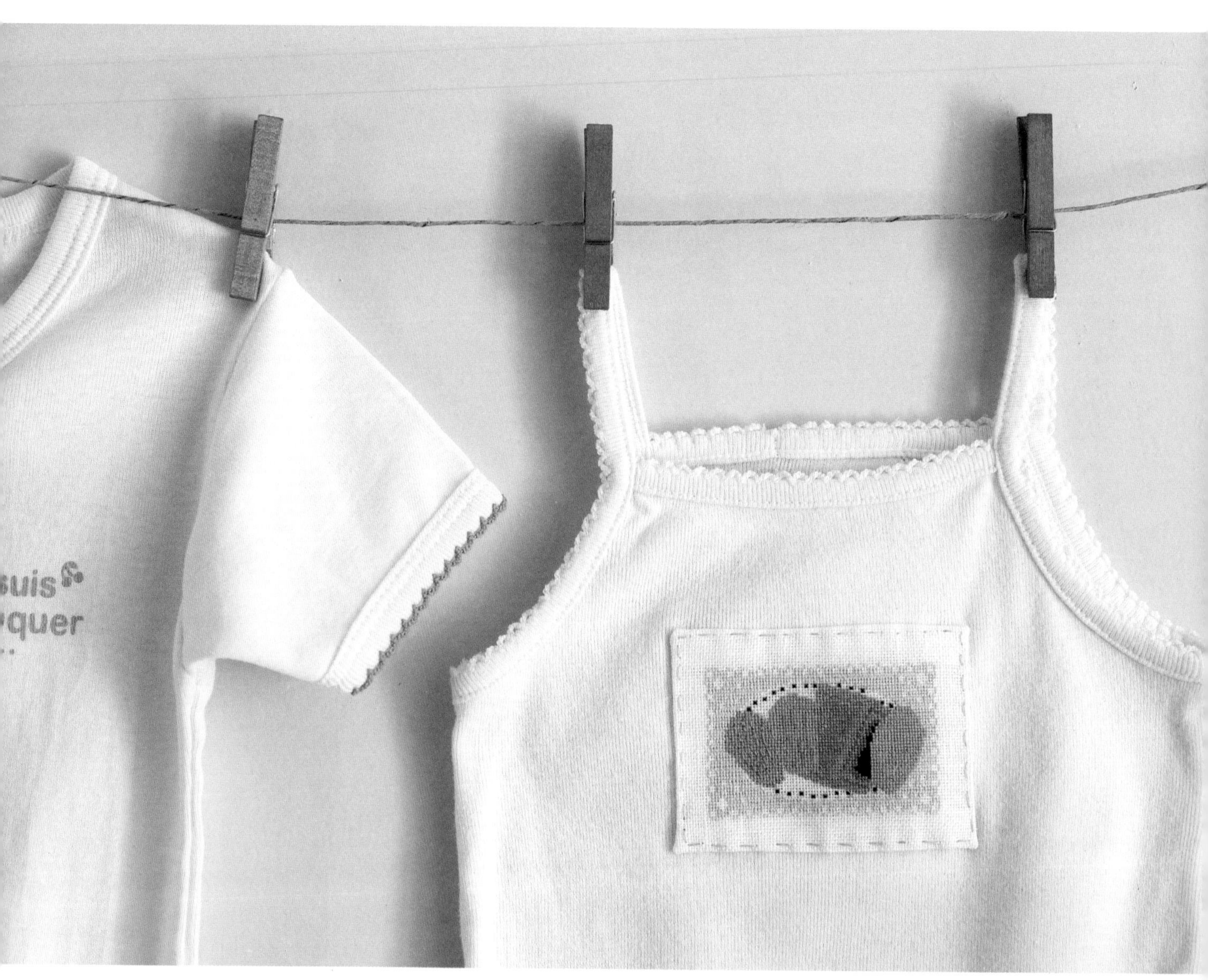

Singlet

instructions page 79
chart page 134

T-shirt

instructions page 80
chart pages 132–133

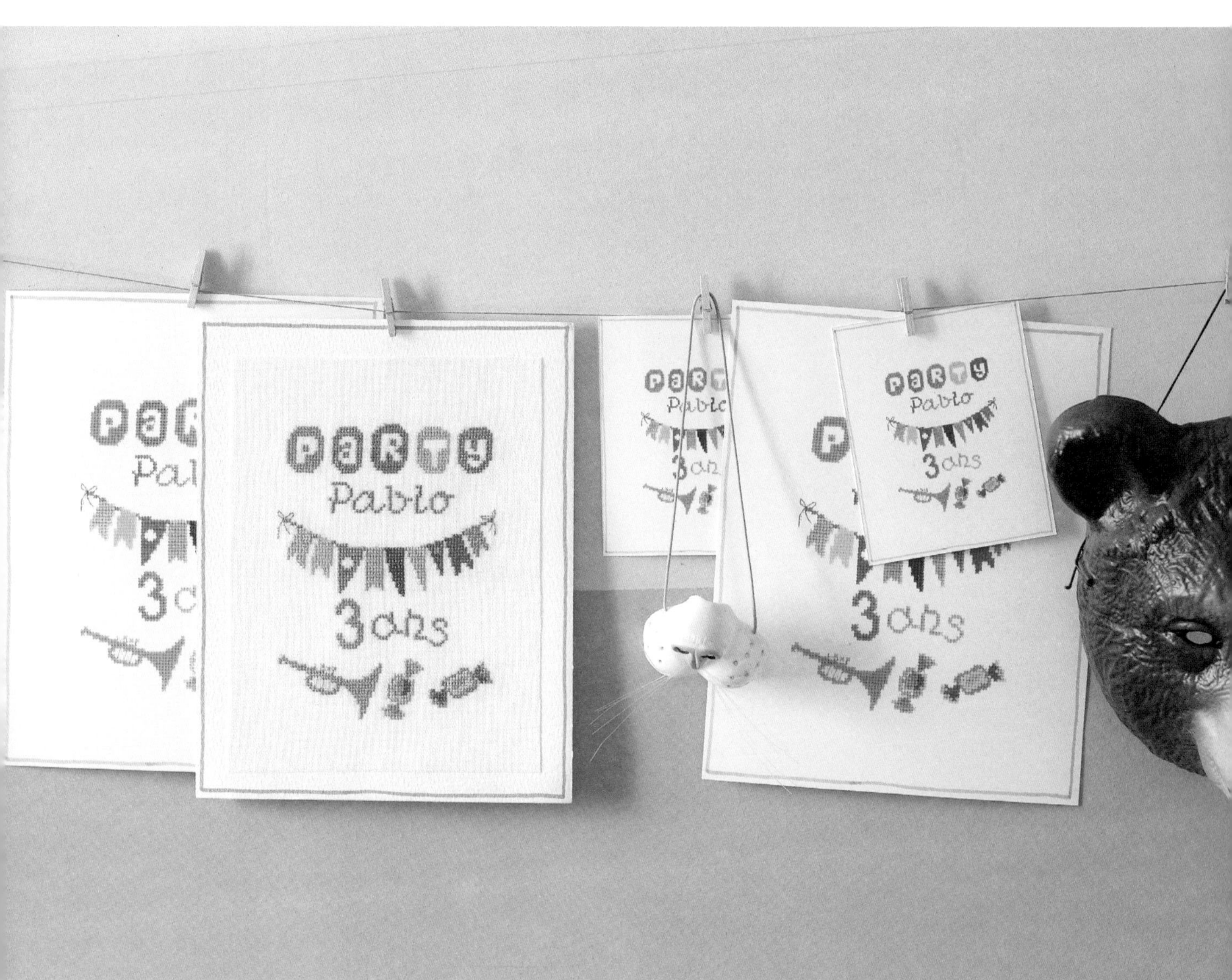

Birthday cards

instructions page 80
charts pages 98–99

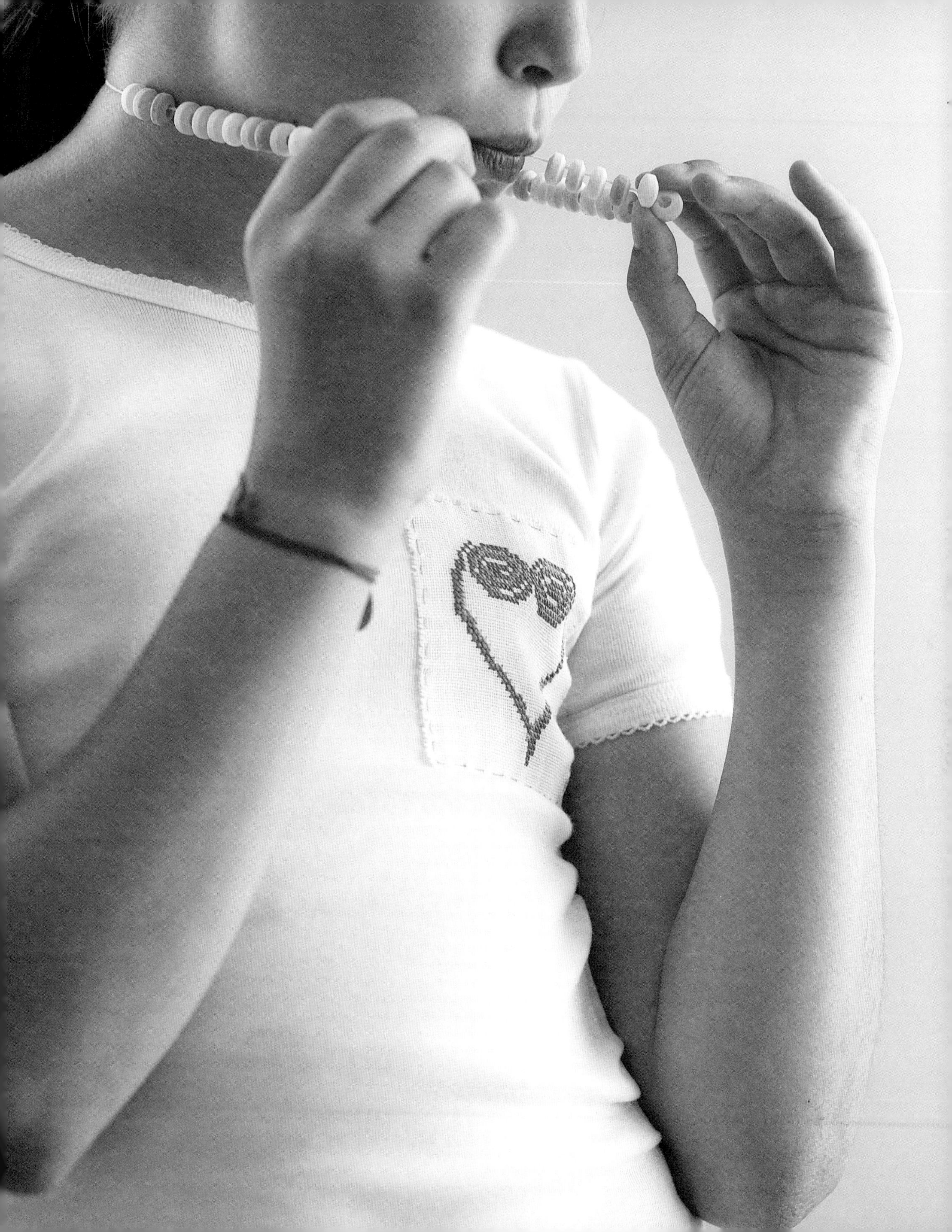

Placemat

instructions page 81
chart pages 136–137

Napkin

instructions page 81
chart pages 136–137

Instructions

Wall hanging – photo page 2 / chart pages 106–107

DMC Mouliné stranded cotton: Blanc (white), 162, 739, 3817, 151, 728, 734, 3045, 159, 3836, 783, 3733, 160, 3790, 161, 902 ✲ cross-stitch and backstitch.

Embroider the 'Plump Round Macarons' design using cross-stitches over 2 threads, leaving a 10 cm edge all around the pattern. Hem the fabric and glue the embroidery to a piece of thin cardboard.

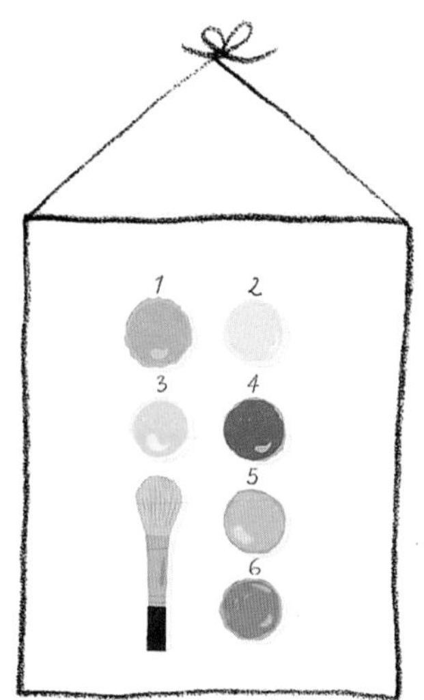

Tablecloth and napkins – photo pages 6–7 / chart pages 86–87

DMC Mouliné stranded cotton: 211, 818, 644, 3689, 728, 503, 760, 3023, 3733, 783, 209 318, 581, 3790, 3816, 602, 349, 317, 3831, 310 ✲ cross-stitch and backstitch.

Embroider, using cross-stitches over 2 threads, five cupcakes in the centre of the tablecloth, then the cherry and strawberry in the centre of a napkin.

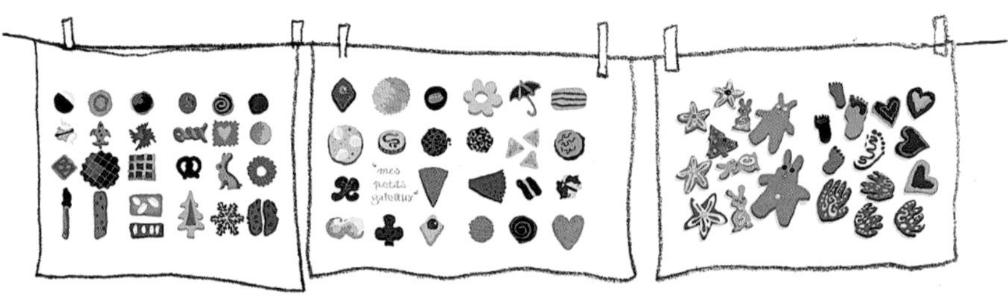

The three gourmands – photo pages 8–9 / charts pages 88–93

DMC Mouliné stranded cotton: 151, 160, 161, 162, 164, 209, 211, 310, 317, 318, 327, 349, 351, 435, 436, 437, 503, 581, 597, 602, 721, 728, 729, 732, 733, 738, 761, 833, 898, 902, 3023, 3032, 3033, 3045, 3052, 3354, 3689, 3726, 3733, 3761, 3766, 3790, 3832, 3836, 3862, 3864 ✲ cross-stitch and backstitch.

Embroider the 3 gourmand designs using cross-stitches over 2 threads, leaving a 6 cm border all around. Carefully fray the threads 2 cm deep all around the edge.

Labels – photo pages 10–11 / charts pages 88–93

DMC Mouliné stranded cotton: 734, 3733, 597, 3816, 320, 208, 3831, 310 ✲ cross-stitch and backstitch.

Embroider the biscuit motifs in the centre of a piece of fabric using cross-stitches over 2 threads, then stick them directly to jars using a little glue.

Bed tidy – photo page 12 / chart pages 94–95

DMC Mouliné stranded cotton: 162, 164, 349, 436, 761, 3023, 3052, 3733, 3836 ✲ cross-stitch and backstitch.

Embroider the numbers in the centre of the fabric using cross-stitches over 2 threads, then make a fairly large pocket for holding toys.

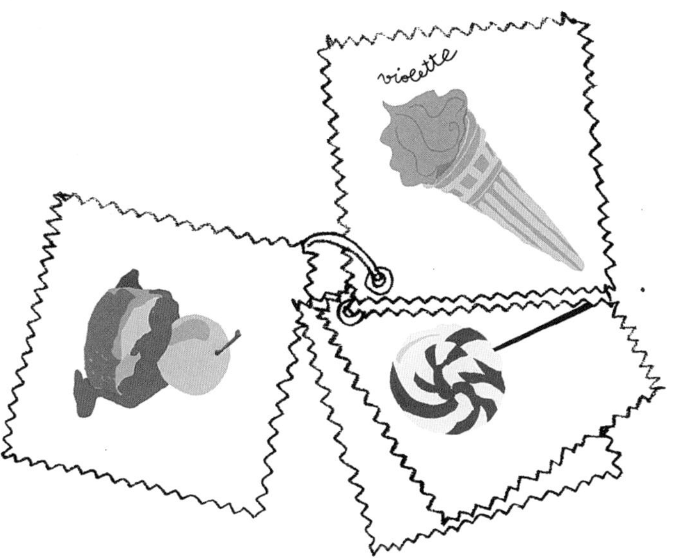

Small toy – photo page 13 / charts pages 94–95 and 132–133

DMC Mouliné stranded cotton: 151, 210, 3045, 209, 436, 208, 3858, 3354, 437, 3733, 833, 310 ✲ cross-stitch.

Embroider four or five small motifs using cross-stitches over 2 threads. Apply some iron-on interfacing to the back then make a hole in the four or five pieces and join them together with a ring.

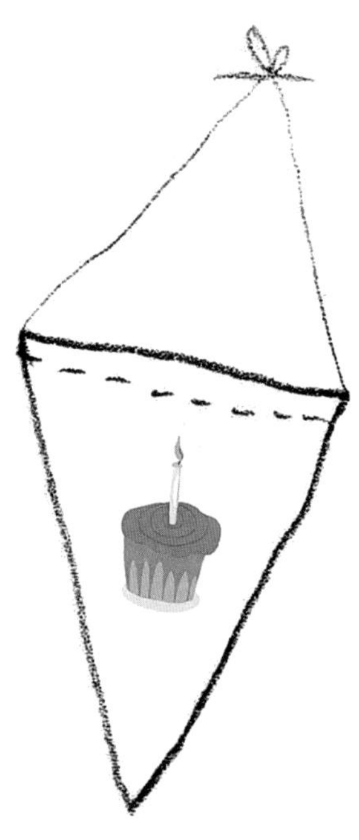

Pennant – photo page 14 / chart pages 96–97

DMC Mouliné stranded cotton: 162, 728, 3045, 738, 721, 351, 3831, 208 ✲ cross-stitch and backstitch.

Make a pennant, then embroider the cake in the centre using cross-stitches over 2 threads.

Notebook – photo page 15 / chart pages 96–97

DMC Mouliné stranded cotton: 151, 519, 734, 993, 3733, 3816, 350, 208 ✲ cross-stitch and backstitch.

Measure the piece of fabric to fit your notebook. Embroider the balloons in the centre of the piece of fabric using cross-stitches over 2 threads, then glue it directly onto the notebook.

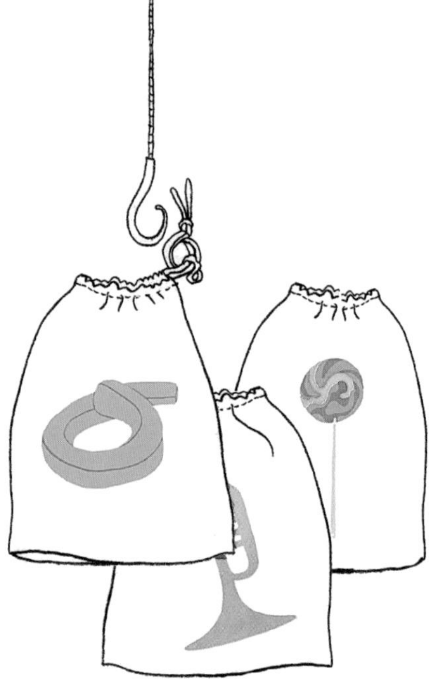

Small bags – photo page 16 / charts pages 96–97 and 100

DMC Mouliné stranded cotton: 151, 519, 761, 760, 597, 3733 ✲ cross- stitch and backstitch.

Embroider three or four motifs using cross-stitches over 2 threads, then make small bags. Sew a small ribbon to each bag to tie it up.

Box – photo page 17 / chart pages 96–97

DMC Mouliné stranded cotton: 162, 351, 728, 519, 3045, 3733, 721, 3772, 996 ✲ cross-stitch and backstitch.

Measure a piece of fabric to fit the box. Embroider a cake in the centre of the piece of fabric using cross-stitches over 2 threads, then glue it directly to the lid of the box.

Baby pants – photo page 18 / chart pages 100–101

DMC Mouliné stranded cotton: 3743, 519, 799, 798, 349 ✲ cross-stitch and backstitch.

Measure a piece of fabric to fit the baby pants before you begin. Embroider a bonbon in the centre of a piece of fabric using cross-stitches over 2 threads, then sew it on to the pair of baby pants.

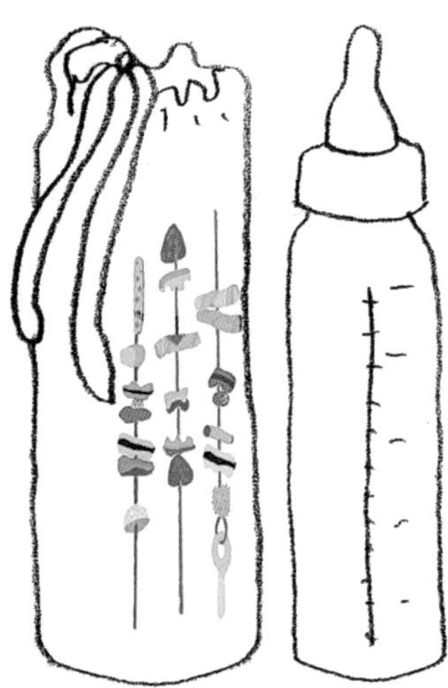

Baby bottle cover – photo page 19 / chart pages 100–101

DMC Mouliné stranded cotton: 3743, 472, 3761, 151, 519, 742, 3354, 3733, 597, 996, 799, 581, 3816, 3862, 721, 209, 602, 3832, 798, 208, 349 ✲ cross-stitch and backstitch.

Measure a piece of fabric to fit the particular bottle. Embroider the motif in the centre of the piece of fabric using cross-stitches over 1 thread, then sew the cover. Finish by sewing on a drawstring to close the bag.

Apron – photo page 20 / chart pages 102–103

DMC Mouliné stranded cotton: Blanc (white), Écru (natural), 3033, 162, 3761, 738, 728, 415, 519, 472, 3045, 729, 160, 783, 3766, 3832, 798, 349 ✲ cross-stitch and backstitch.

Measure out enough fabric to make an apron. Embroider the 'Crêpes Party' chart in the top centre of the piece of fabric using cross-stitches over 2 threads. Attach two long ties to each end to make the apron strings.

Variation: in the same way as the apple pie project (photo on page 50), embroider the crêpes recipe in the centre of a piece of fabric then glue it to a frame.

Heat-mat – photo page 21 / chart pages 102–103

DMC Mouliné stranded cotton: Blanc (white), Écru (natural), 3033, 162, 3761, 738, 415, 160, 783, 349 ✲ cross-stitch and backstitch.

Embroider a detail from the 'Crêpes Party' chart in the centre of a small square or rectangle of fabric using cross-stitches over 2 threads, then sew it on to a heat-resistant mat.

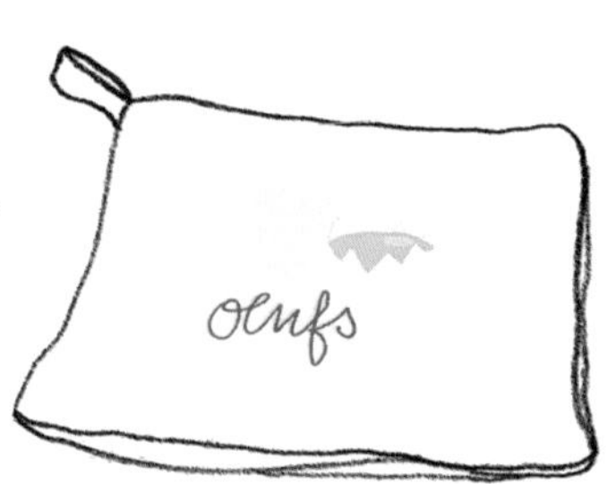

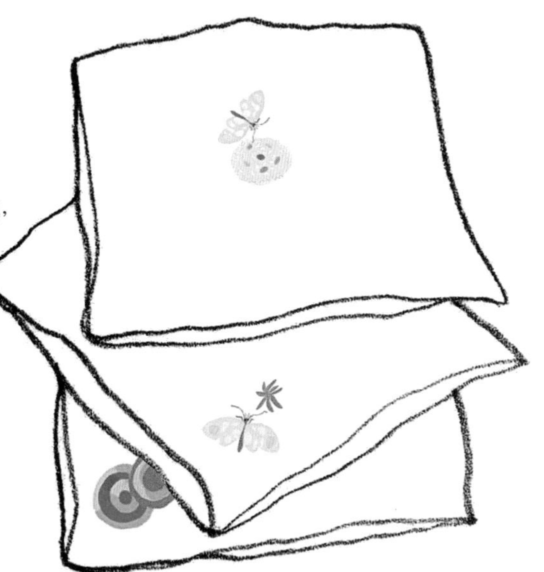

Three cushions – photo pages 22–23 / chart pages 104–105

DMC Mouliné stranded cotton: 3743, 822, 3743, 3354, 519, 834, 3755, 3733, 833, 320, 721, 602, 3862, 349, 3831, 902 ✲ cross-stitch and backstitch.

Embroider details from the 'Tea Time' chart in different positions on pieces of fabric cut to make cushions, using cross-stitches over 2 threads, then stuff the cushions and sew together.

Macaron bag – photo page 24 / chart pages 106–107

DMC Mouliné stranded cotton: Blanc (white), 162, 739, 151, 728, 734, 3733, 738, 733, 3778, 3790, 3832, 3835, 902 ✲ cross-stitch and backstitch.

Measure out enough fabric to make a small, medium or large bag. Embroider the macarons in the centre of a piece of fabric using cross-stitches over 2 threads, then make a bag.

Cloth case – photo page 25 / chart pages 106–107

DMC Mouliné stranded cotton: 739 ✲ cross-stitch and backstitch.

Embroider the motif in the centre of a piece of fabric using cross-stitches over 2 threads, then make a pocket. Finish by inserting a zipper.

Tea cosy – photo page 26 / chart pages 108–109

DMC Mouliné stranded cotton: 211, 818, 157, 151, 210, 3023, 209, 3790, 208, 3832 ✲ cross-stitch and backstitch.

Embroider the *religieuse* profiterole cake in the centre of a piece of fabric using cross-stitches over 2 threads, then make a tea cosy.

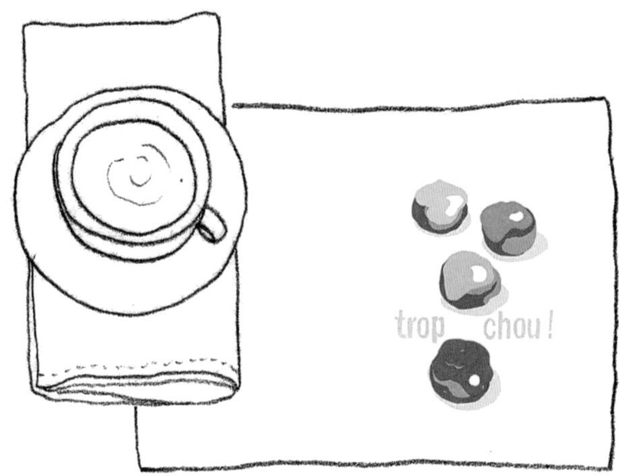

Placemat – photo page 27 / chart pages 108–109

DMC Mouliné stranded cotton: 211, 818, 157, 3761, 151, 519, 734, 761, 760, 3790, 3862 ✲ cross-stitch and backstitch.

Embroider the 'Trop chou!' ('Too cute!') motif in the centre-right section of the placemat using cross-stitches over 2 threads.

Chef's toque – photo page 28 / chart pages 110–111

DMC Mouliné stranded cotton: 162, 3354, 503, 834, 3864, 3861, 581, 3772, 3862, 3860, 3858, 898, 902 ✲ cross-stitch and backstitch.

Embroider the little chocolates in the centre of some linen banding, then sew it on to a toque hat.

'Attention aux moustaches' ('Watch out for moustaches!') napkin – photo page 29 / chart page 139

DMC Mouliné stranded cotton: 644, 3045, 3862, 3832, 3858, 898 ✲ cross-stitch and backstitch.

Embroider the 'attention aux moustaches' ('watch out for moustaches') chart in the centre of a napkin using cross-stitches over 2 threads.

'Trop bon!' ('Too good!') napkin – photo page 30 / chart pages 104–105

DMC Mouliné stranded cotton: 3743, 3354, 834, 902 ✲ cross-stitch and backstitch.

Embroider the cake in the centre of a napkin using cross-stitches over 2 threads.

'Carrément chocolat!' ('Absolutely chocolate!') napkin – photo page 31 / chart pages 110–111

DMC Mouliné stranded cotton: 162, 3033, 151, 3354, 210, 3045, 3864, 435, 581, 434, 3862, 3790, 349, 898, 902, 310 ✲ cross-stitch and backstitch.

Embroider the 'carrément chocolat!' design using cross-stitches over 2 threads, leaving a 10 cm border all around. Hem and glue the embroidery to a piece of thin cardboard.

Tote bag – photo page 32 / chart pages 112–113

DMC Mouliné stranded cotton: Écru (natural), 3743, 677, 162, 3761, 151, 738, 3354, 3733, 729, 3806, 351, 3862, 3832, 349, 3831 ✲ cross-stitch and backstitch.

Measure a piece of fabric large enough to make your bag. Embroider the strawberry shortcake in the centre of a piece of fabric using cross-stitches over 2 threads, then make the tote bag.

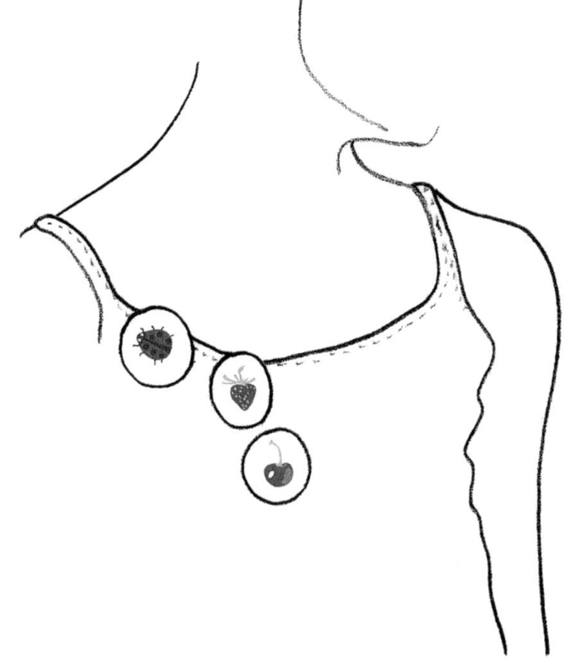

Badges – photo page 33 / charts pages 112–113 and 134

DMC Mouliné stranded cotton: 993, 3733, 959, 351, 3832, 349, 3831 ✲ cross-stitch and backstitch.

Embroider small motifs in the centre of small fabric remnants then make the badges. Embroider the motifs using cross-stitches over 1 thread so they are pretty.

Little girl dress – photo page 34 / chart pages 114–115

DMC Mouliné stranded cotton: 151, 3354, 437, 3733, 833, 310 ✲ cross-stitch and backstitch.

Embroider an ice-cream cone in the centre of a small remnant of fabric using cross-stitches over 2 threads, then sew it onto the dress.

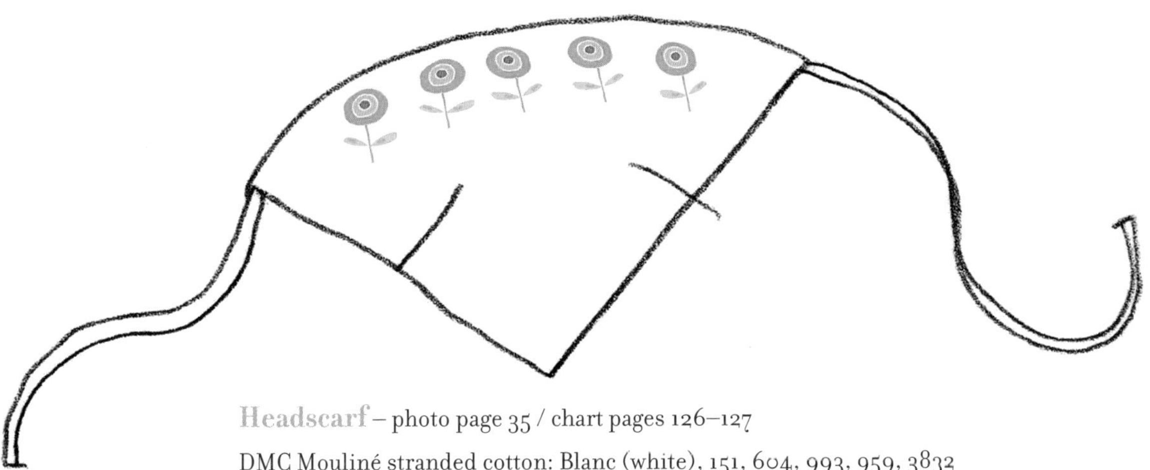

Headscarf – photo page 35 / chart pages 126–127

DMC Mouliné stranded cotton: Blanc (white), 151, 604, 993, 959, 3832
✲ cross-stitch and backstitch.

Embroider small flowers along the longest side of the headscarf using cross-stitches over 2 threads.

Bunting – photo page 36 / chart pages 116–117

DMC Mouliné stranded cotton: 162, 799, 349, 798, 3831
✲ cross- stitch.

Embroider a boiled sweet in the centre of each pre-cut pennant then join them together with a length of thin fancy braid.

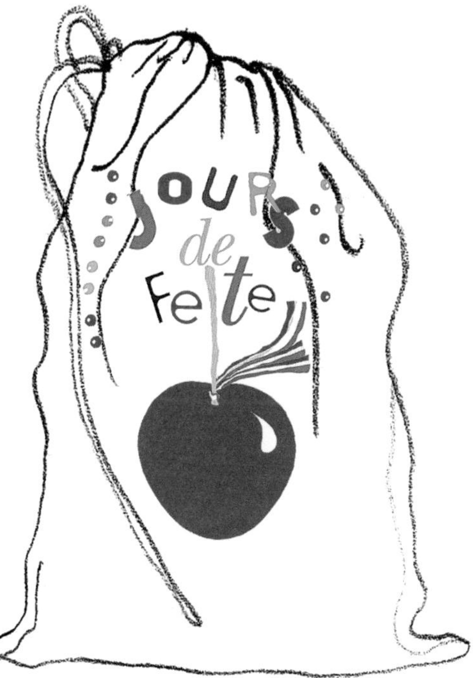

Big bag – photo page 37 / chart pages 116–117

DMC Mouliné stranded cotton: 162, 415, 799, 318, 435, 3815, 349, 798, 3831, 3350, 326, 310 ✲ cross-stitch.

Embroider the 'jours de fête' ('celebration days') motif in the centre of a large piece of fabric using cross-stitches over 2 threads, then make a sack. Finish by attaching a drawstring to close.

Bib – photo page 38 / chart pages 118–119

DMC Mouliné stranded cotton: 162, 3689, 597, 733, 160, 3862, 310 ✲ cross-stitch and backstitch.

Embroider the rabbit in the centre of a bib using cross-stitches over 2 threads.

Medium bag – photo page 39 / chart pages 118–119

DMC Mouliné stranded cotton: 822, 739, 834, 833, 209, 3862, 310 ✲ cross-stitch and backstitch.

Embroider a bell in the centre of a piece of fabric using cross-stitches over 2 threads, then make a bag. Finish by making a drawstring to close.

Eclair tea towel – photo page 40 / chart pages 120–121

DMC Mouliné stranded cotton: 644, 151, 519, 761, 3782, 760, 799, 3862, 3832 ✲ cross-stitch and backstitch.

Embroider the small biscuits in the bottom middle section of a tea towel using cross-stitches over 2 threads.

Chair cover – photo page 41 / chart pages 120–121

DMC Mouliné stranded cotton: 162, 644, 519, 728, 799, 3839, 349 ✲ cross-stitch and backstitch

Embroider a cup and teapot on a chair cover using cross-stitches over 2 threads.

Letter and number games – photo page 42 / chart pages 122–123

DMC Mouliné stranded cotton: 644, 211, 3761, 3325, 734, 210, 3733, 760, 728, 519, 3045, 3778, 597, 3832, 349, 310 ✲ cross-stitch and backstitch.

Embroider the letter and number tables using cross-stitches over 2 threads, leaving a 10 cm border all around. Hem the pieces and glue to pieces of thin cardboard.

Equation cushion – photo page 43 / chart pages 122–123

DMC Mouliné stranded cotton: 210, 3733, 519, 3832, 310 ✲ cross- stitch and backstitch.

Measure out the fabric to make a cushion.Embroider a message, equation or riddle in the top centre of the piece of fabric using cross-stitches over 2 threads, then stuff and sew the cushion.

Pocket tidy – photo page 44 / chart pages 124–125

DMC Mouliné stranded cotton: 162, 3761, 644, 472, 677, 3689, 210, 3325, 3766, 728, 834, 993, 3733, 415, 160, 318, 741, 3806, 581, 721, 3790, 3832, 349, 798, 902, 310 ✲ cross-stitch and backstitch.

Embroider five details from the chart on separate small pieces of fabric. Hem all around the embroidered pieces then sew them on to a tea towel to make pockets.

Jar – photo page 45 / chart pages 124–125

DMC Mouliné stranded cotton: 162, 3761, 644, 3766, 834, 993, 3733, 741, 581, 721, 902, 310 ✲ cross-stitch and backstitch.

Embroider the cups using cross-stitches over 2 threads, then make a jar-cover.

Announcement card – photo page 46 / chart pages 126–127

DMC Mouliné stranded cotton: Blanc (white), 162, 728, 3761, 151, 604, 993, 729, 959, 3806, 3832, 310 ✲ cross-stitch and backstitch.

Embroider the tiered cake on a piece of fabric using cross-stitches over 1 thread, then attach it to a piece of thin cardboard. You can photocopy or scan the embroidery to send it as a wedding announcement.

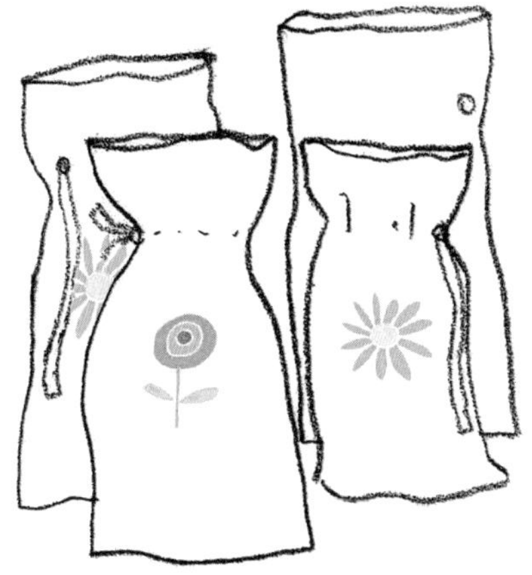

Lolly bags – photo page 47 / chart pages 126–127

DMC Mouliné stranded cotton: Blanc (white), 728, 151, 604, 993, 729, 959 ✲ cross-stitch and backstitch.

Embroider three or four motifs on small pieces of fabric using cross-stitches over 2 threads, then sew together the lolly bags. Attach a thin ribbon to make a drawsting or tie.

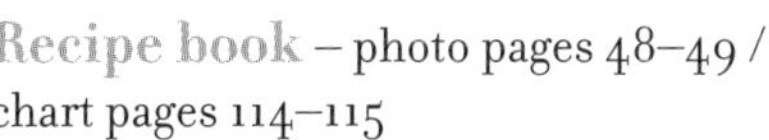

Recipe book – photo pages 48–49 / chart pages 114–115

DMC Mouliné stranded cotton: 151, 3354, 3733, 760, 799, 798, 310 ✲ cross-stitch and backstitch.

Embroider the ice-cream sundae and 'tres frais!!!' ('very cool!!!') motif in the centre of a piece of fabric using cross-stitches over 2 threads, then glue it to a ring binder.

Apple pie wall hanging – photo page 50 / chart pages 128–129

DMC Mouliné stranded cotton: Blanc (white), 162, 3761, 3689, 738, 210, 519, 728, 834, 993, 159, 783, 729, 209, 597, 3816, 435, 3862, 602, 349, 310 ✲ cross-stitch and backstitch.

Embroider the apple pie recipe in the centre of a piece of fabric, cut to fit the frame of your choice. Then glue the fabric to the frame.

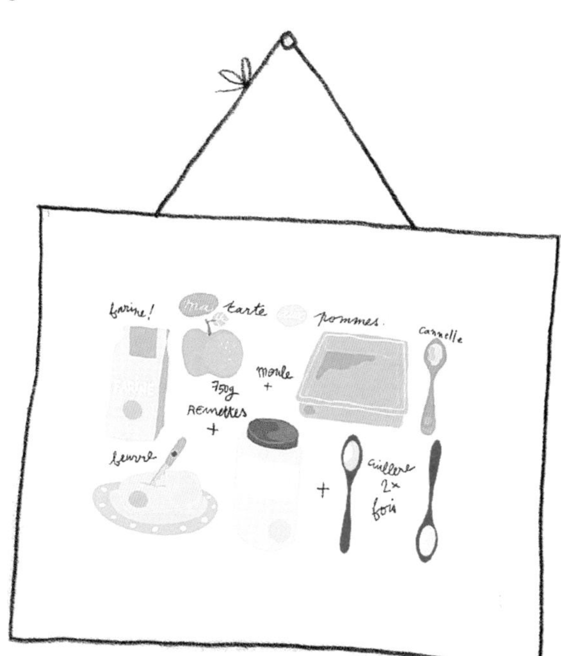

Apple tea towel – photo page 51 / chart pages 128–129

DMC Mouliné stranded cotton: Blanc (white), 3761, 210, 993, 3816, 435, 310 ✲ cross-stitch and backstitch.

Embroider a detail in one of the bottom corners of a tea towel using cross- stitches over 2 threads.

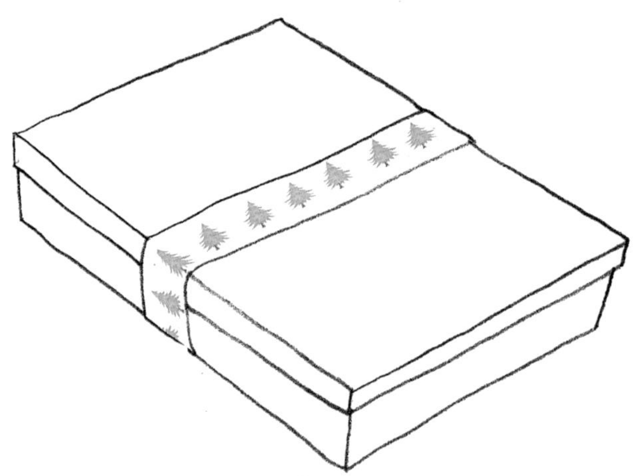

Gift ribbon – photo page 52 / chart pages 130–131

DMC Mouliné stranded cotton: 3761, 519, 597, 435 ✲ cross- stitch and backstitch.

Embroider the frieze of pine trees onto a ribbon using cross-stitches over 2 threads. Repeat the frieze as many times as needed to make the right length.

Gift tags – photo page 53 / chart pages 130–131

DMC Mouliné stranded cotton: 162, 3761, 519, 3733, 833, 3816, 435, 3832, 349, 310 ✲ cross-stitch and backstitch.

Embroider the Christmas motifs using cross-stitches over 2 threads. Apply some iron-on interfacing to the back then make a hole in the embroidered pieces to thread through a tie.

Handkerchief – photo page 54 / chart pages 100–101

DMC Mouliné stranded cotton: 472, 3761, 151, 519, 3354, 3733, 996, 799, 351, 3832, 208 ✲ cross-stitch and backstitch.

Embroider the lolly bracelet in the right corner of a handkerchief using cross-stitches over 1 thread.

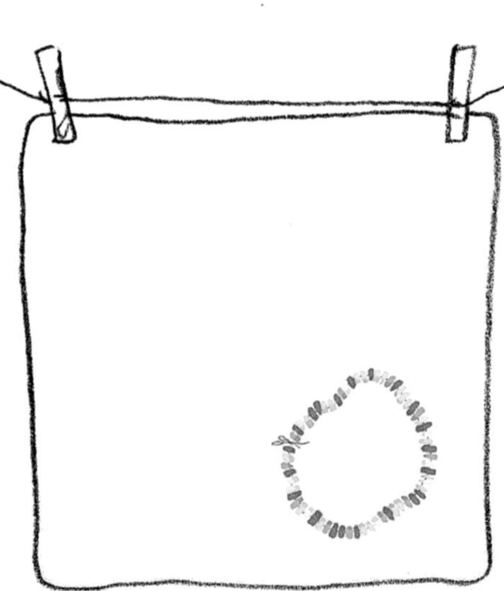

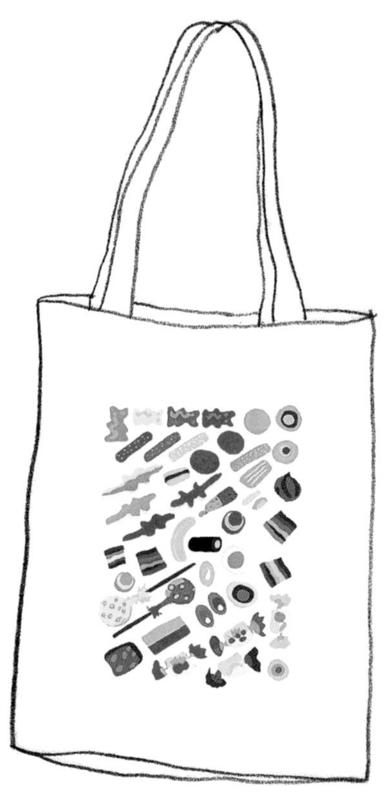

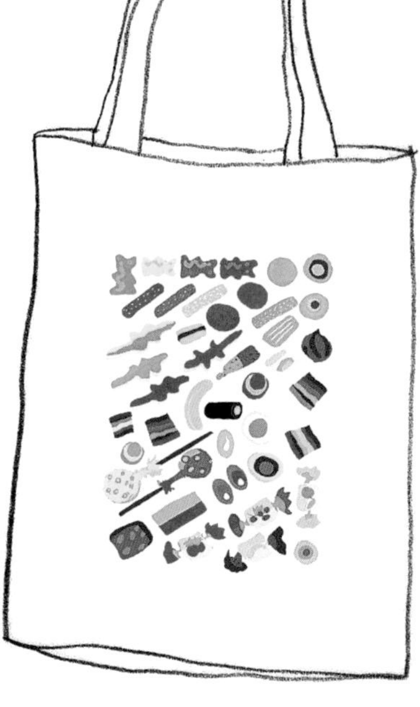

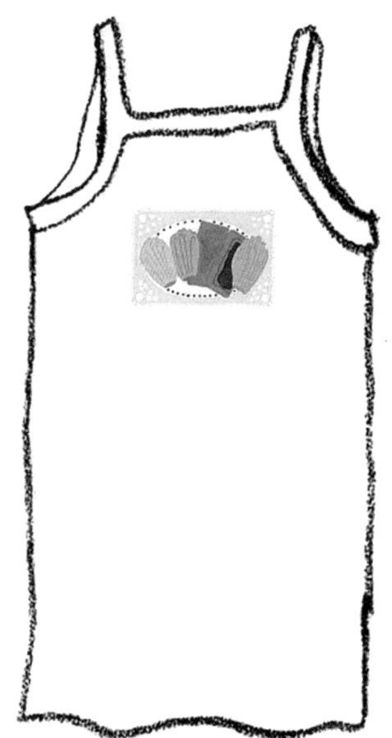

Singlet – photo page 56 / chart page 134

DMC Mouliné stranded cotton: 162, 3045, 436, 733, 3778, 3861, 3772, 3860, 310 ✲ cross-stitch and backstitch.

Embroider the madeleines on a small piece of fabric using cross-stitches over 1 thread. Hem the piece, then sew it on to a singlet.

Small shoulder bag – photo page 55 / chart pages 132–133

DMC Mouliné stranded cotton: 677, 162, 472, 3761, 151, 519, 728, 3354, 503, 993, 3045, 783, 996, 799, 3733, 581, 3816, 721, 209, 320, 3832, 602, 161, 208, 349, 902, 310 ✲ cross-stitch and backstitch.

Embroider the collection of bonbons using cross-stitches over 1 thread, then make a small bag.

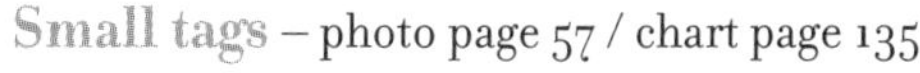

Small tags – photo page 57 / chart page 135

DMC Mouliné stranded cotton: 3354, 761, 415, 3733, 760, 318, 414 ✲ cross-stitch and backstitch.

Embroider the cookie-cutter motifs on pieces of fabric using cross-stitches over 2 threads, then glue them to some paper or cardboard tags.

Birthday cards – photo page 58 / chart pages 98–99

DMC Mouliné stranded cotton: 162, 151, 728, 734, 519, 210, 993, 3733, 3045, 742, 760, 597, 799, 209, 3816, 721, 581, 3772, 3832, 208 ✲ cross-stitch and backstitch.

Embroider the birthday design, using cross-stitches over 2 threads, personalising it using the alphabet and numbers in the chart on pages 84–85. You can then photocopy or scan it and make birthday party invitations.

T-shirt – photo page 59 / chart pages 132–133

DMC Mouliné stranded cotton: 209, 161, 208 ✲ cross-stitch.

Embroider the heart on a piece of fabric using cross-stitches over 2 threads. Hem the piece then sew it onto the upper right section of a T-shirt.

Placemat – photo page 60 / chart pages 136–137

DMC Mouliné stranded cotton: 739, 437, 783, 435, 3832, 798, 310 ✲ cross-stitch.

Embroider the croissant on the left side of a placemat using cross-stitches over 2 threads, positioning it in the centre.

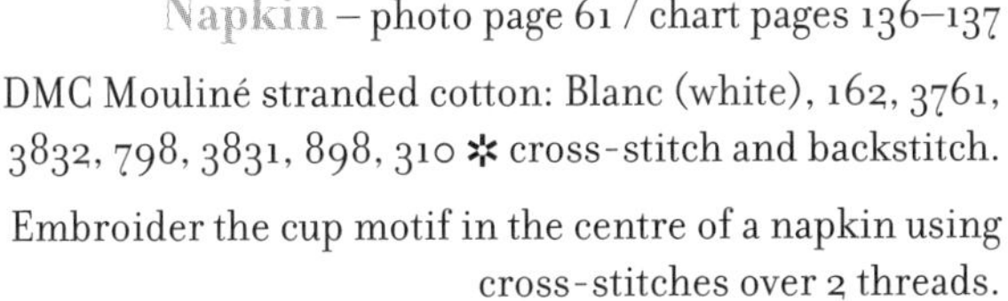

Napkin – photo page 61 / chart pages 136–137

DMC Mouliné stranded cotton: Blanc (white), 162, 3761, 3832, 798, 3831, 898, 310 ✲ cross-stitch and backstitch.

Embroider the cup motif in the centre of a napkin using cross-stitches over 2 threads.

'C'est chic' wall hanging – photo page 142 / chart page 138

DMC Mouliné stranded cotton: 162, 151, 3761, 210, 209, 3766, 3810, 208, 327 ✲ cross-stitch.

Embroider the design in the centre of the fabric using cross- stitches over 2 threads. The fabric can be used as a wall hanging.

Charts

For making mouth-watering words...

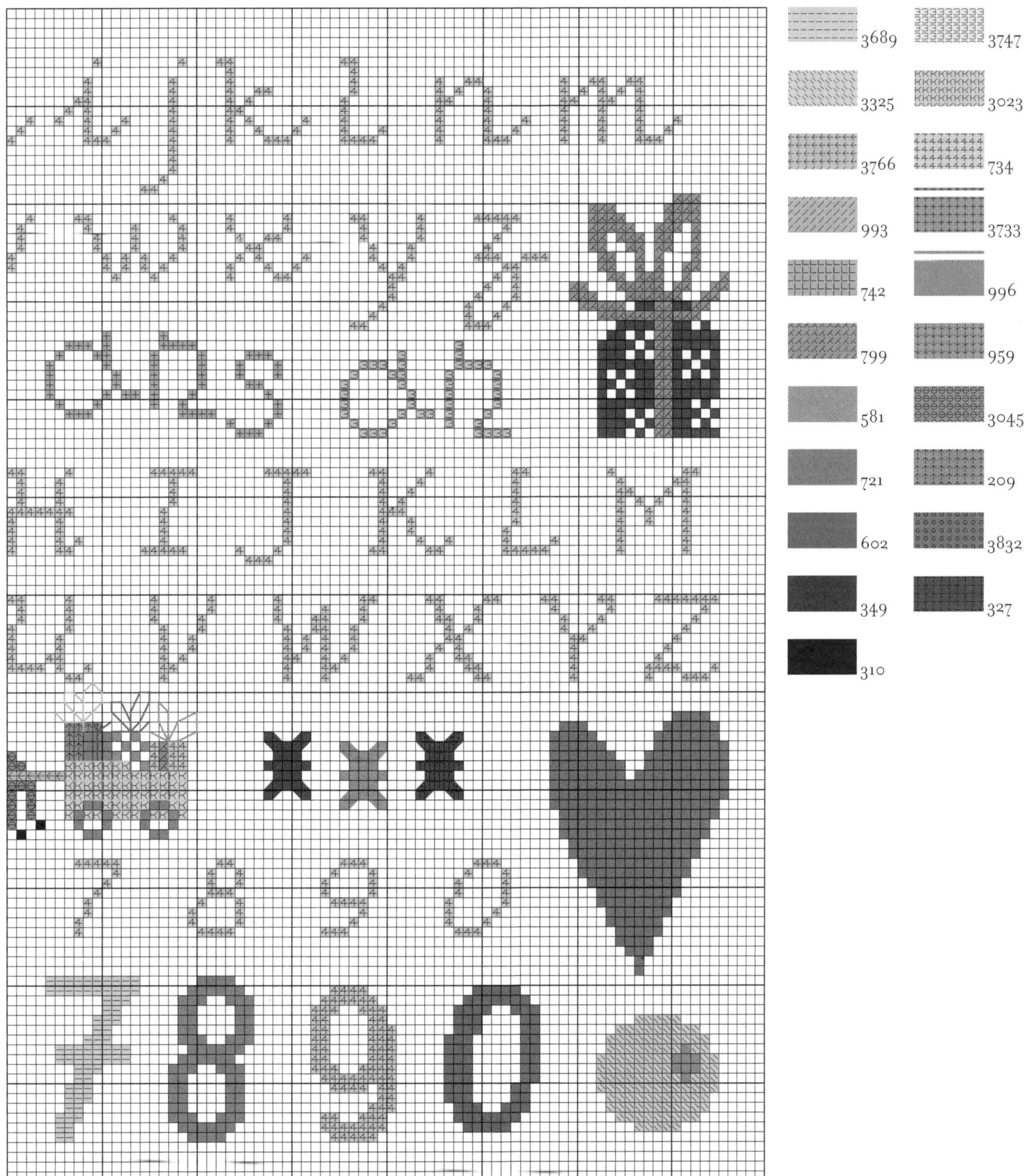
3689
3747
3325
3023
3766
734
993
3733
742
996
799
959
581
3045
721
209
602
3832
349
327
310

Cupcakes / photos pages 6–7

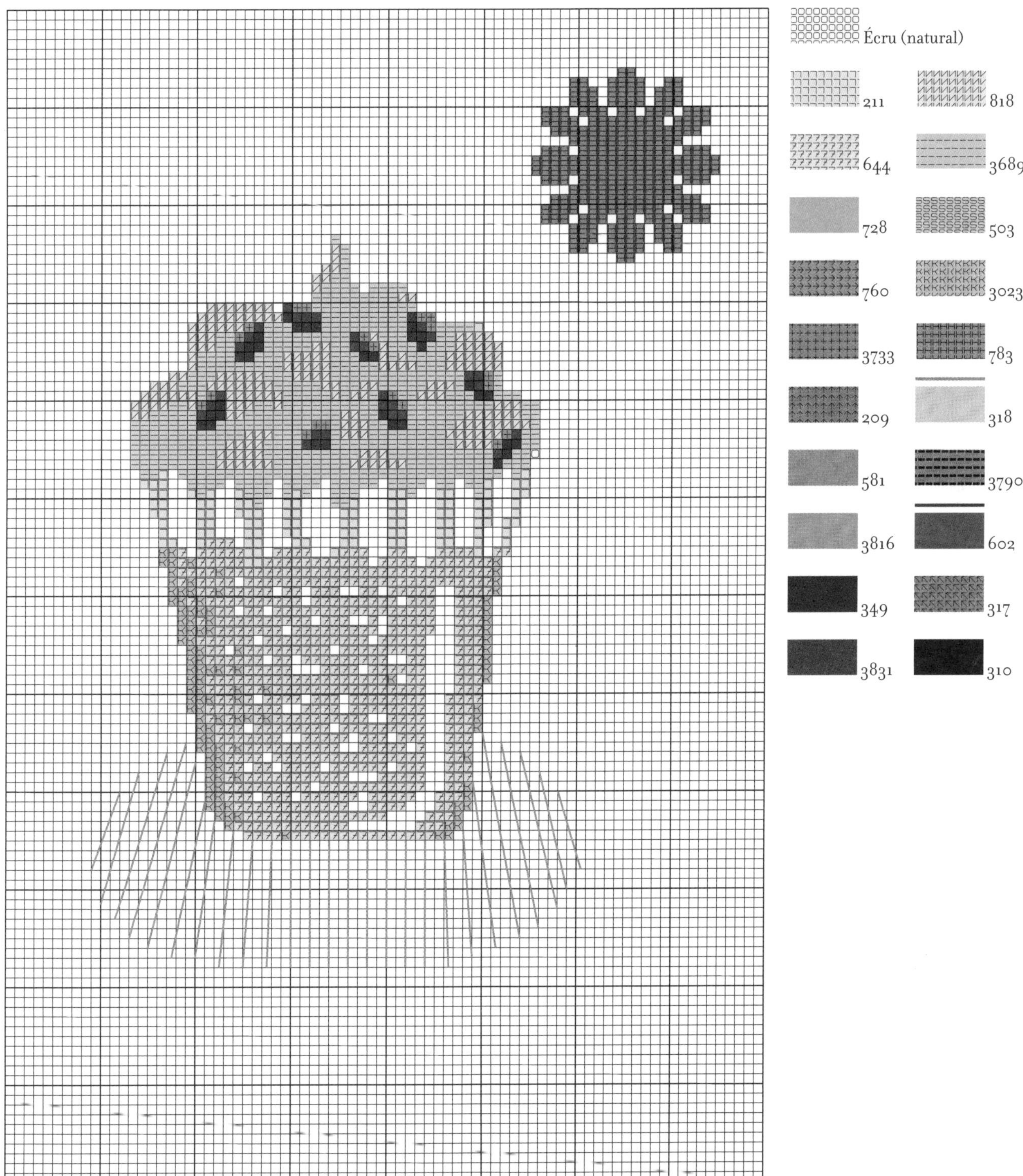
Écru (natural)
211
818
644
3689
728
503
760
3023
3733
783
209
318
581
3790
3816
602
349
317
3831
310

Biscuits, shortbreads and cookies / photos pages 8–9 and 10–11

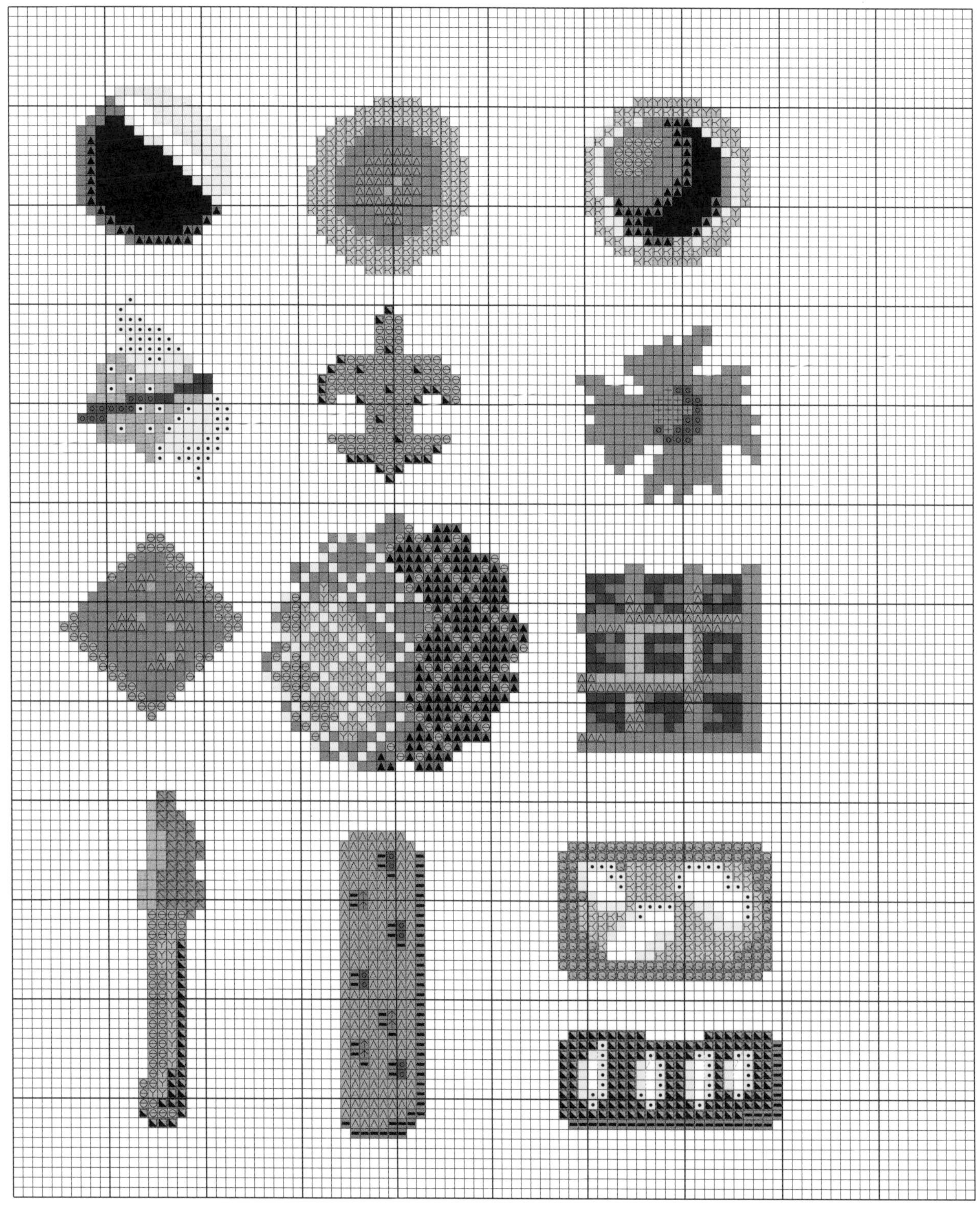

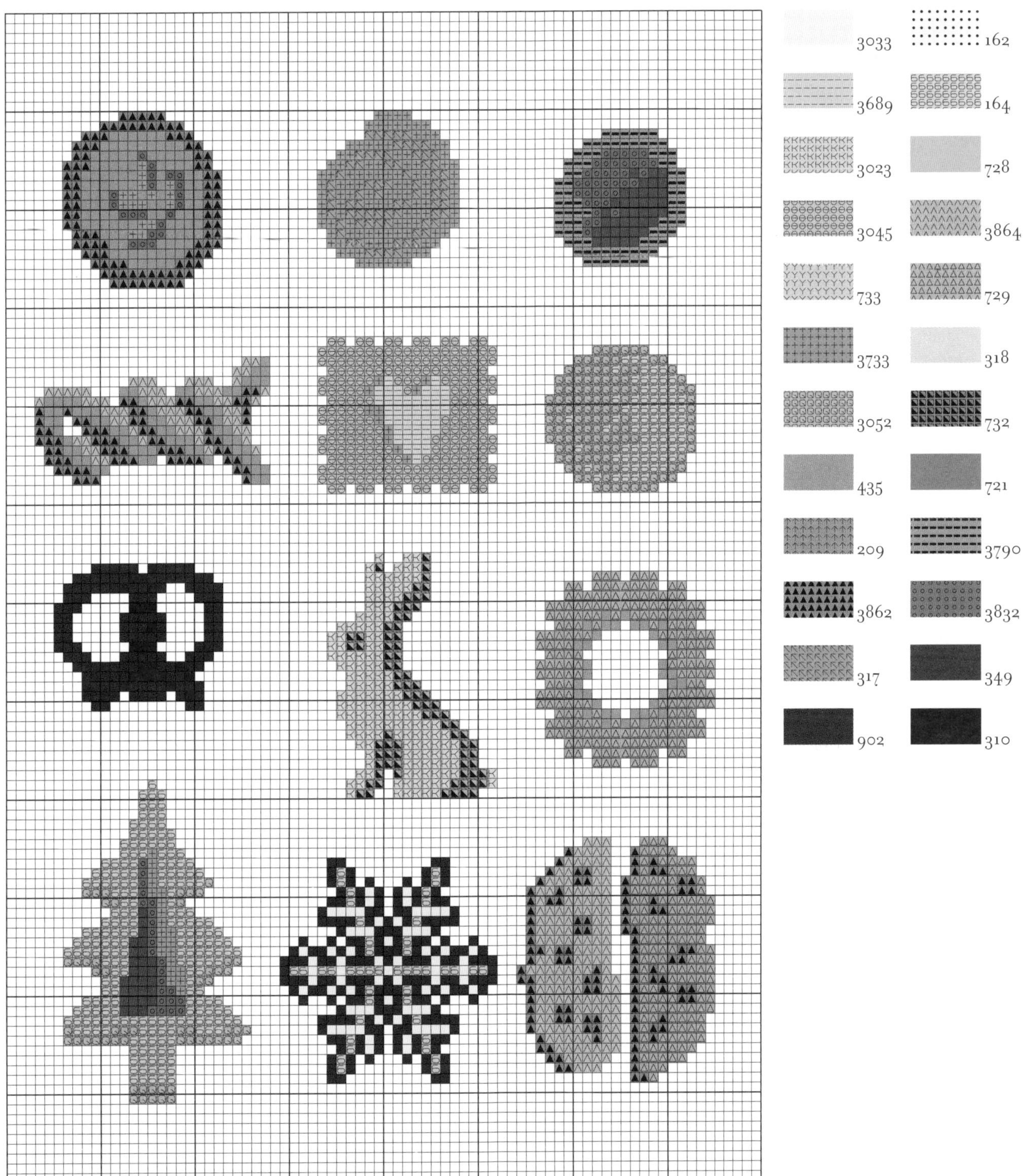

3033
162
3689
164
3023
728
3045
3864
733
729
3733
318
3052
732
435
721
209
3790
3862
3832
317
349
902
310

More biscuits, shortbreads and cookies / photos pages 8–9 and 10–11

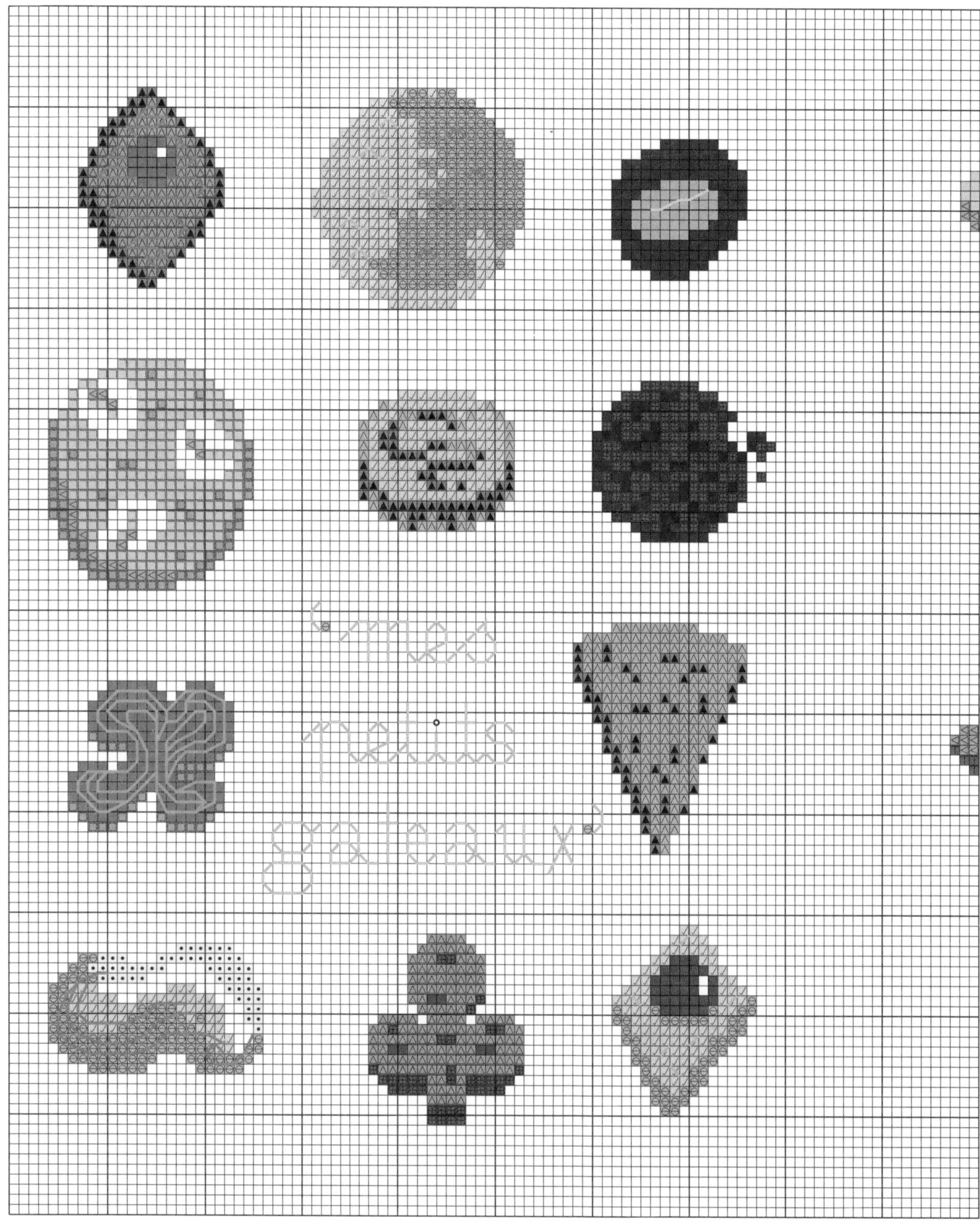

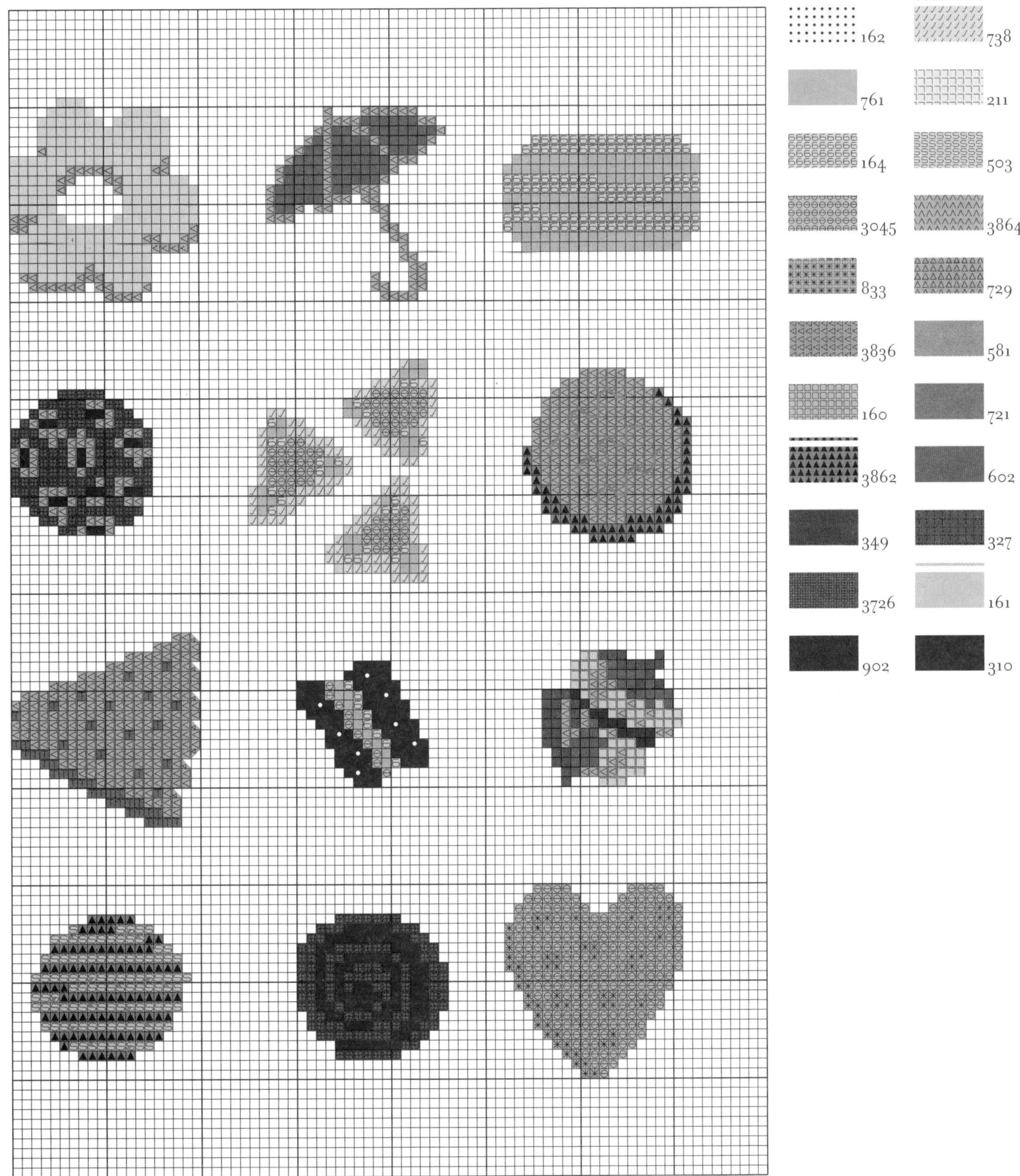
162
738
761
211
164
503
3045
3864
833
729
3836
581
160
721
3862
602
349
327
3726
161
902
310

More biscuits, shortbreads and cookies / photos pages 8–9 and 10–11

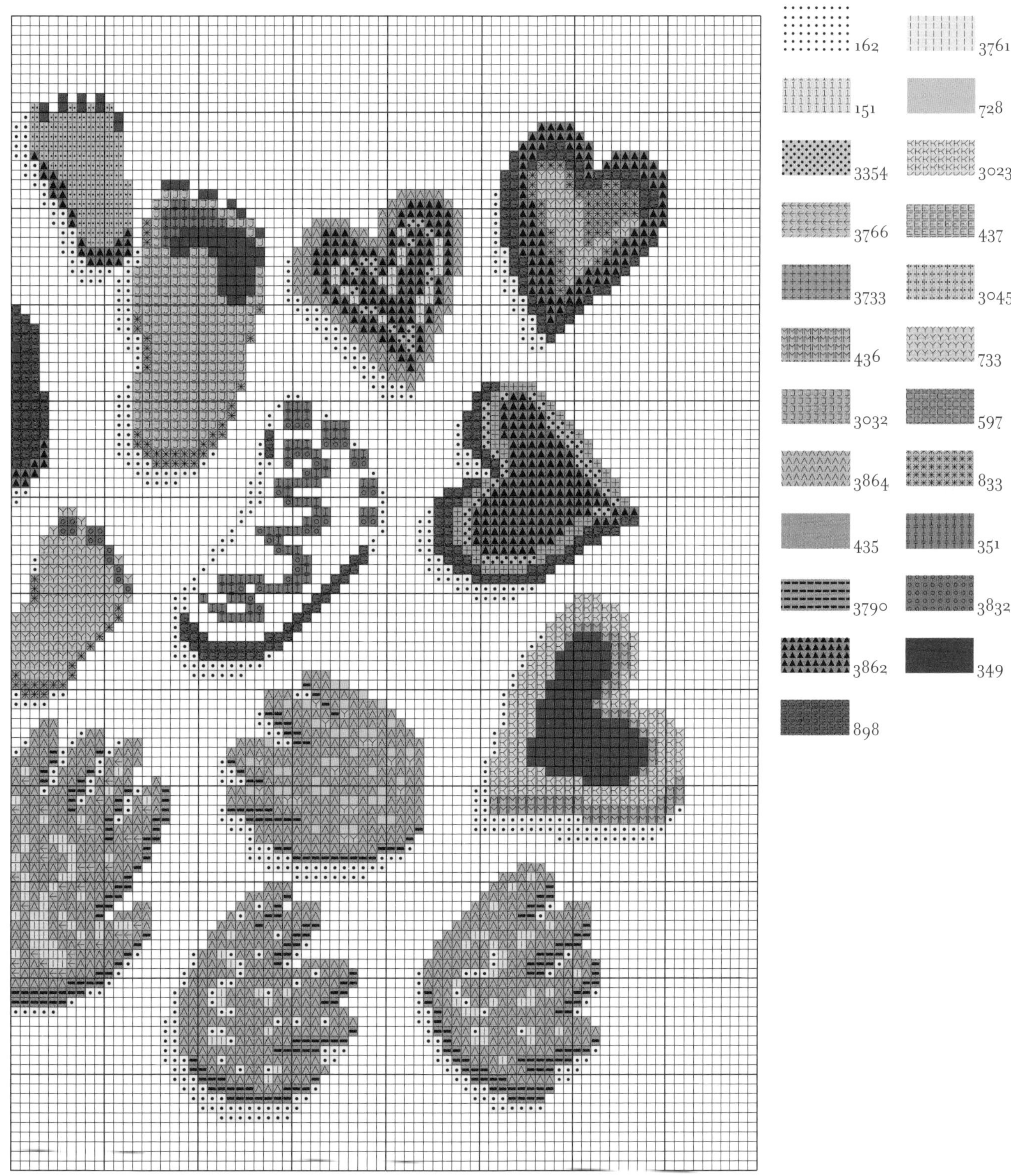
162
3761
151
728
3354
3023
3766
437
3733
3045
436
733
3032
597
3864
833
435
351
3790
3832
3862
349
898

‘Cueillir des cerises’ (‘Picking cherries’) / photos pages 12–13

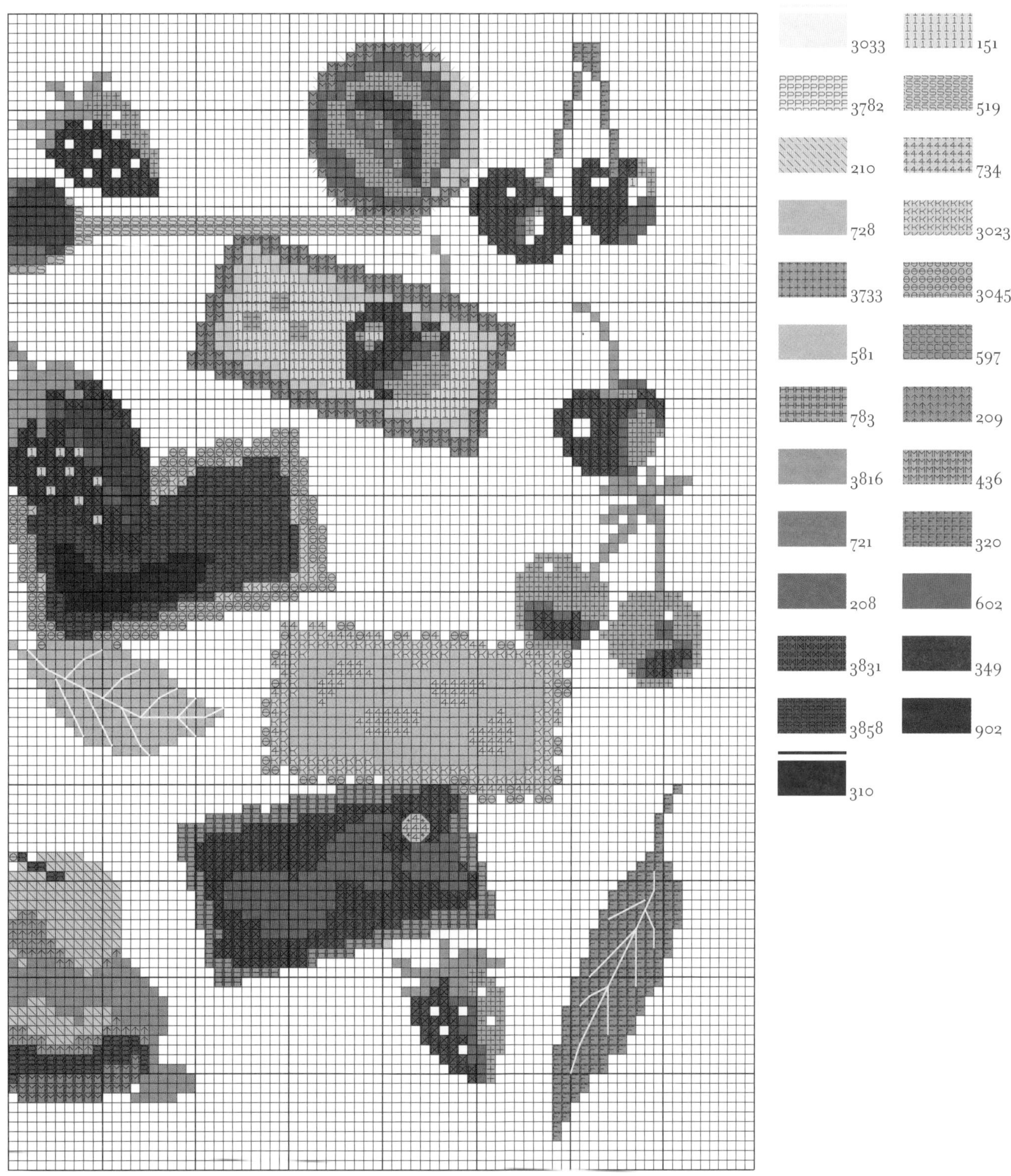

3033
151
3782
519
210
734
728
3023
3733
3045
581
597
783
209
3816
436
721
320
208
602
3831
349
3858
902
310

Birthday party! / photos pages 14, 15, 17 and 58

162
151
728
519
210
734
3045
993
3733
783
581
597
209
3816
3806
721
3772
351
996
3831
208
349

Birthday party! (continued) / photos pages 16, 17 and 58

162
151
728
734
519
210
993
3733
3045
742
760
597
799
209
3816
721
581
3772
3832
208

Lolly shop / photos pages 16 and 18–19

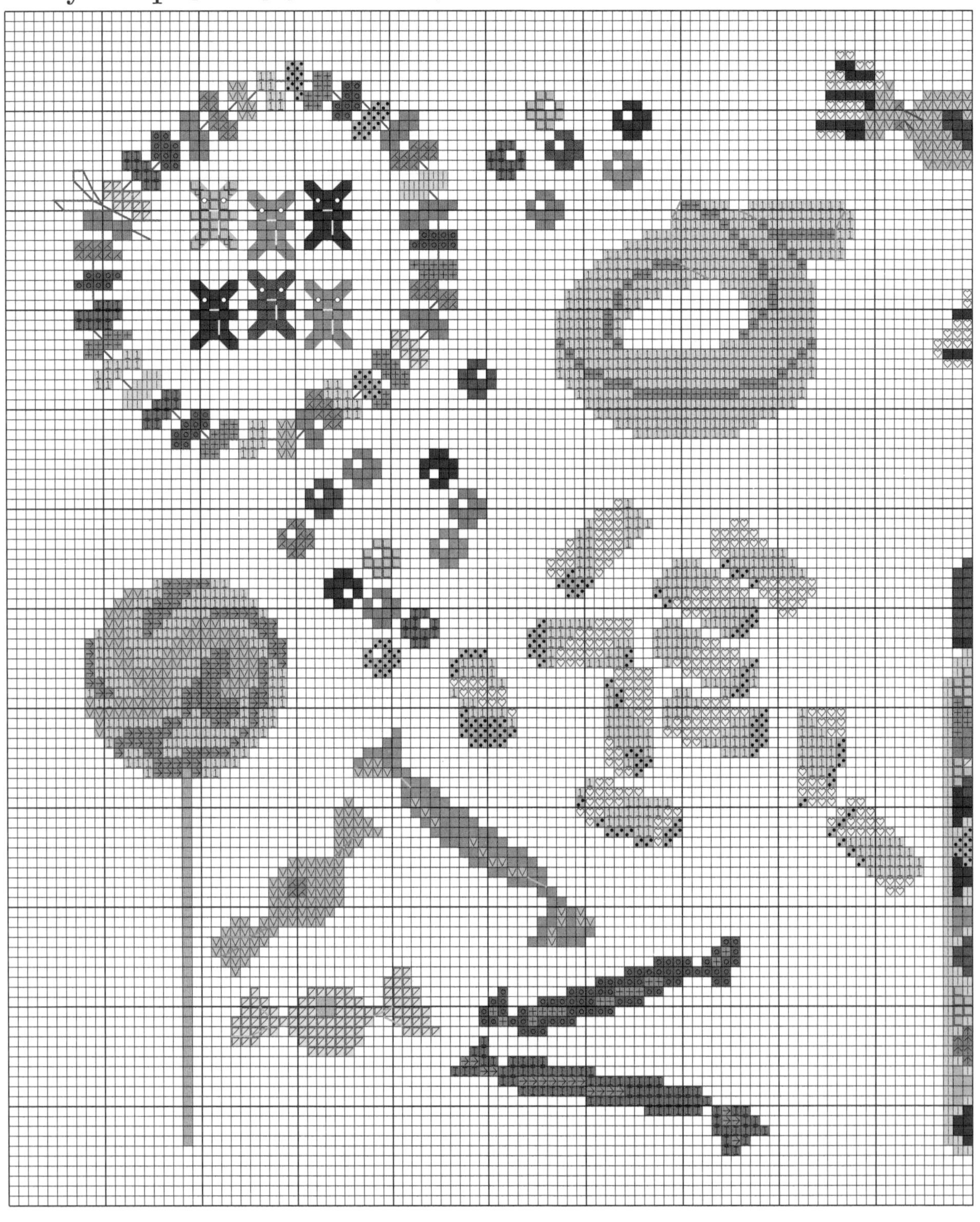

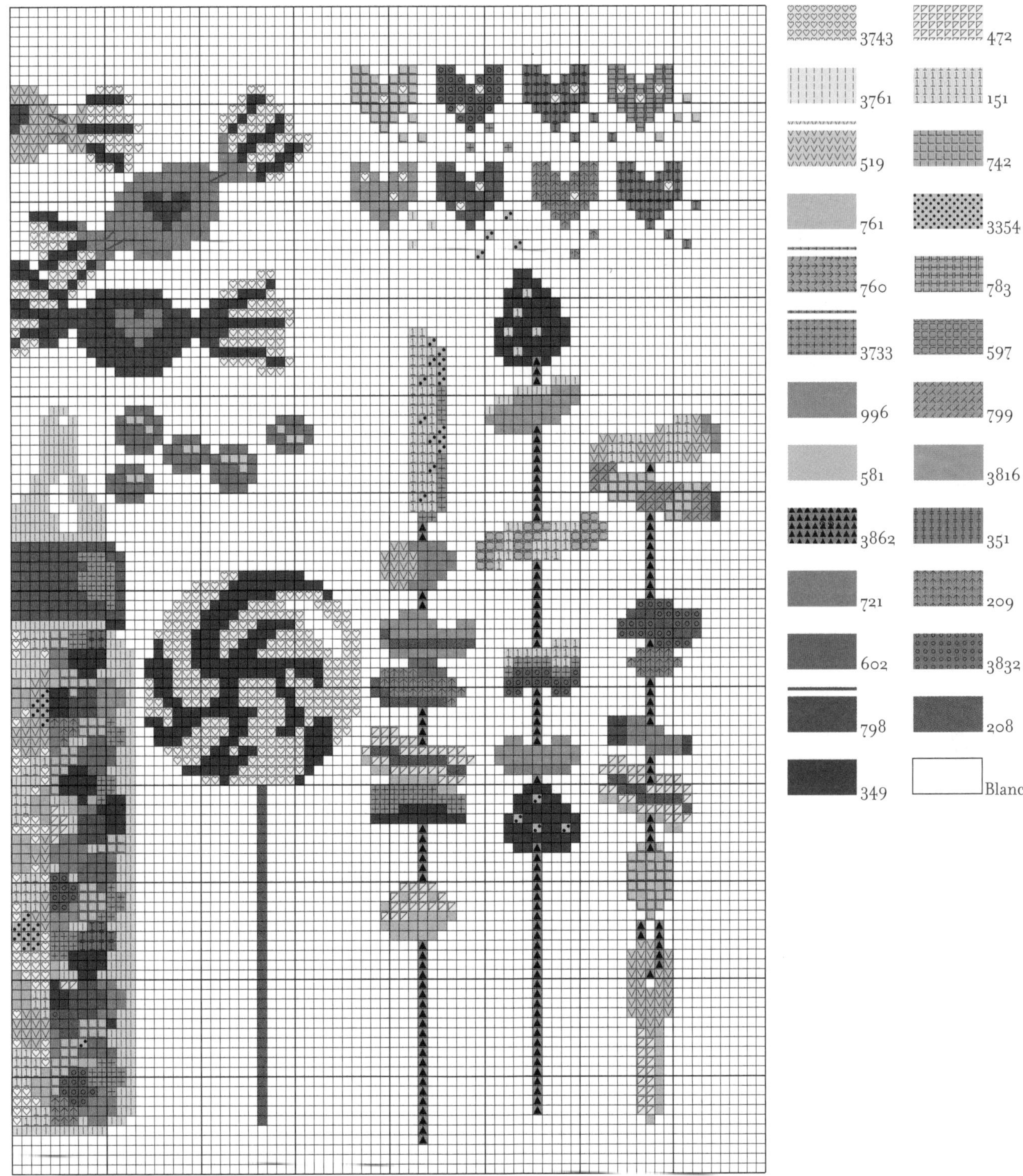
3743
472
3761
151
519
742
761
3354
760
783
3733
597
996
799
581
3816
3862
351
721
209
602
3832
798
208
349
Blanc

Crêpes party / photos pages 20–21

Blanc
Écru
3033
162
3761
738
728
415
519
472
3045
729
160
783
3766
3832
798
349

Tea time / photos pages 22–23 and 30

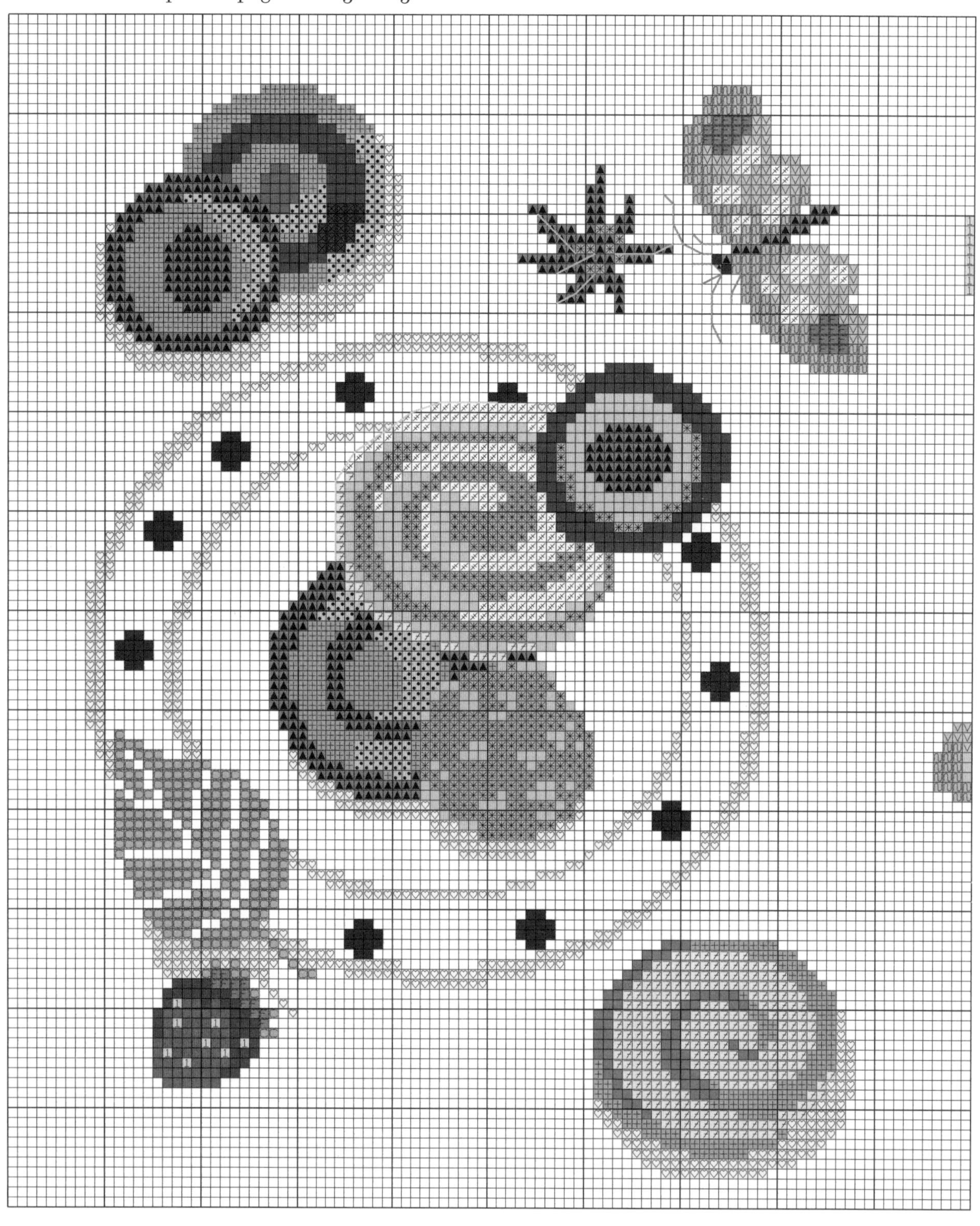

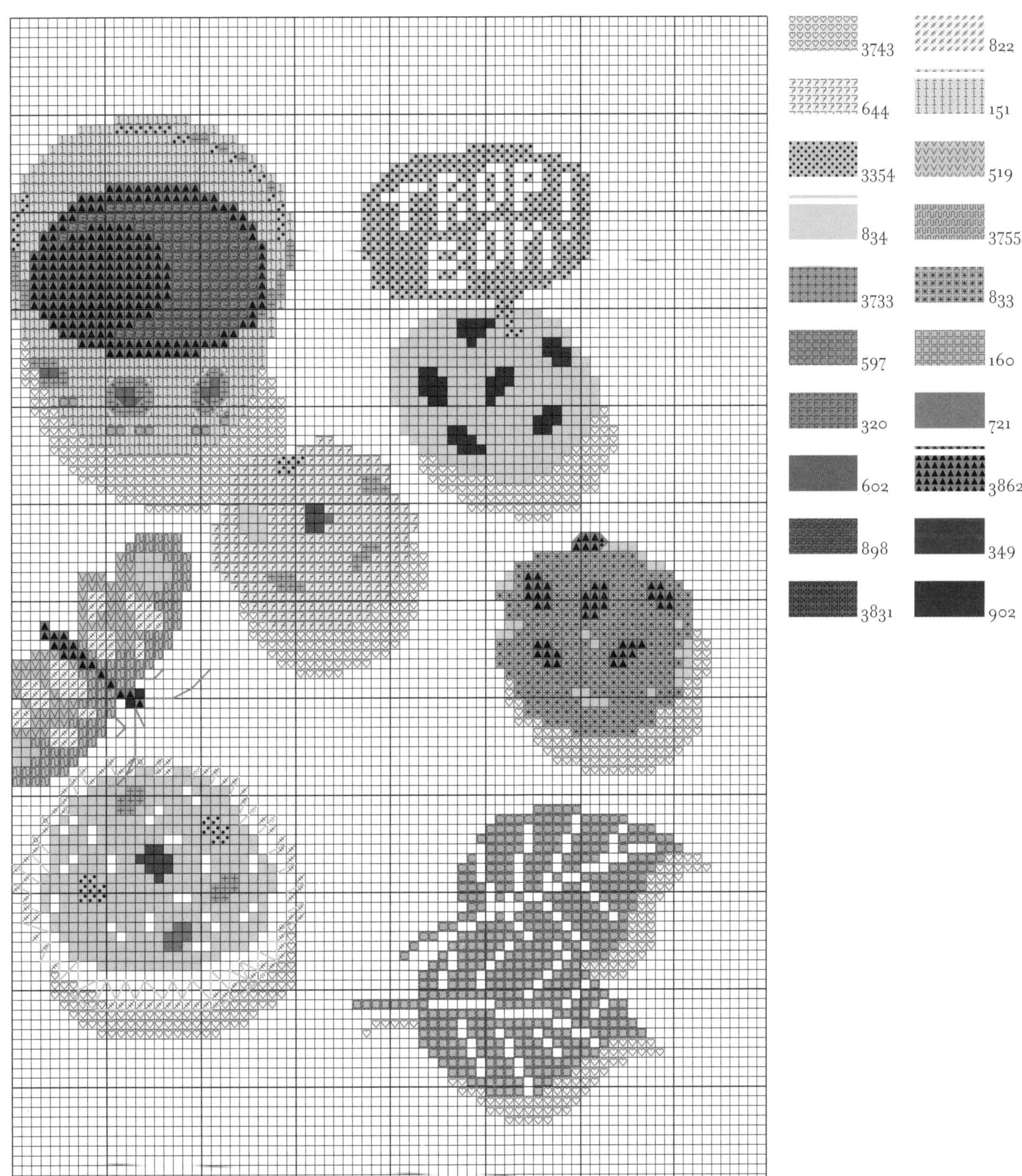
3743
822
644
151
3354
519
834
3755
3733
833
597
160
320
721
602
3862
898
349
3831
902

Plump round macarons / photos pages 2 and 24–25

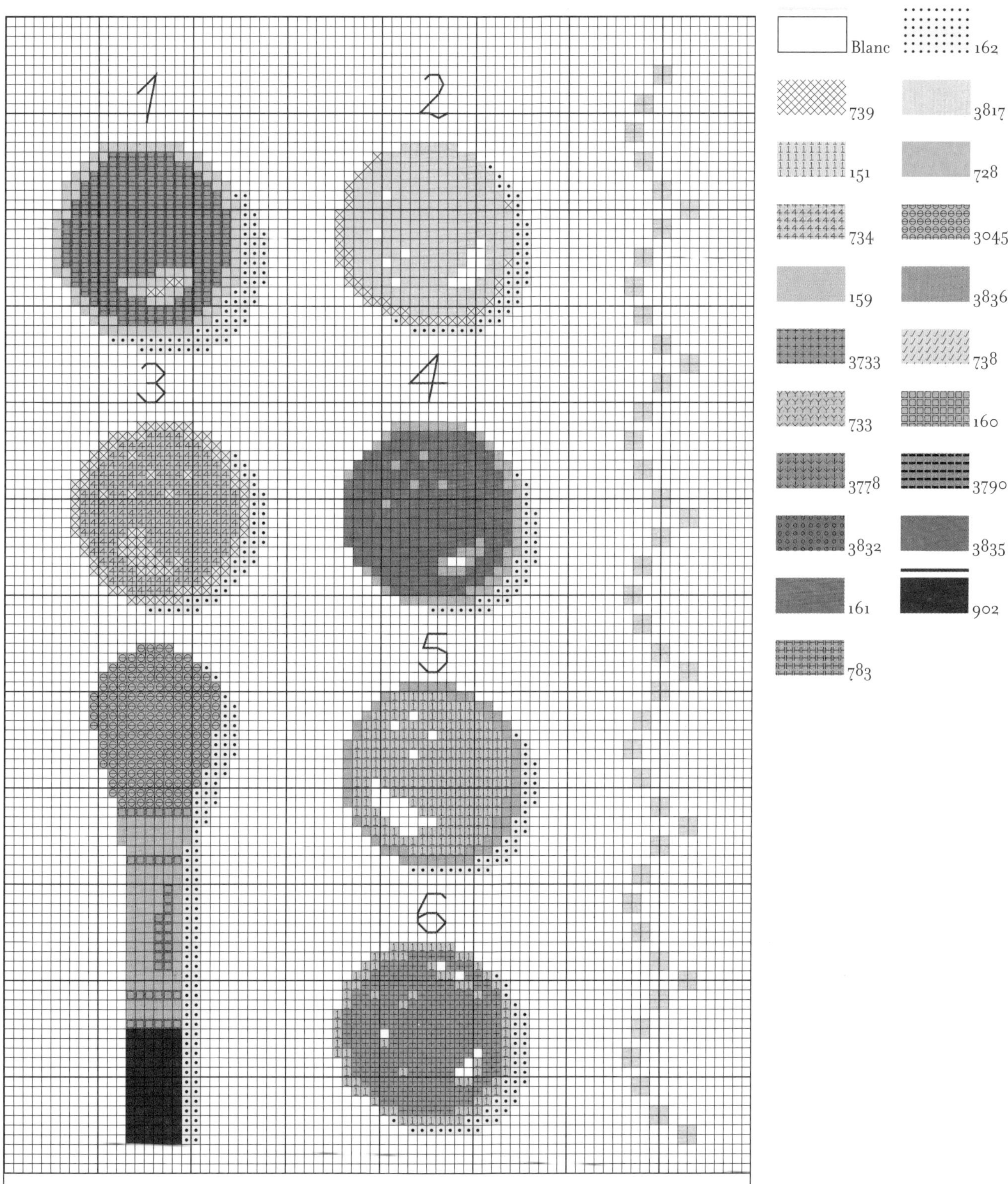
1
2
3
4
5
6
Blanc
162
739
3817
151
728
734
3045
159
3836
3733
738
733
160
3778
3790
3832
3835
161
902
783

'Trop chou!' ('Too cute!') / photos pages 26–27

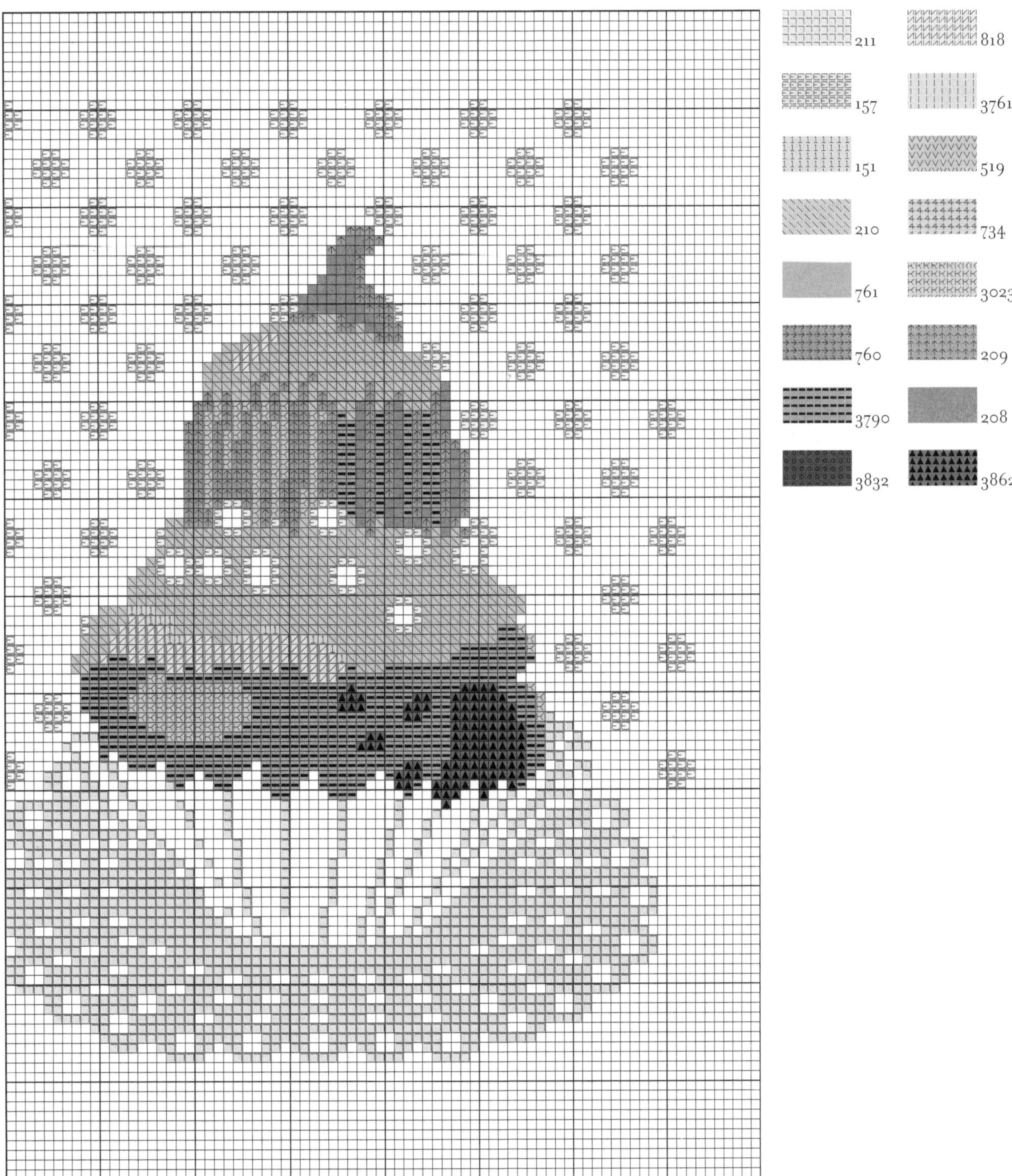
211
818
157
3761
151
519
210
734
761
3023
760
209
3790
208
3832
3862

'Carrément chocolat' ('Absolutely chocolate') / photos pages 28 and 31

162
3033
151
3354
210
503
3045
834
3864
833
435
3861
581
3772
434
3862
3860
3790
3858
349
898
902
310

Strawberry shortcake / photos pages 32–33

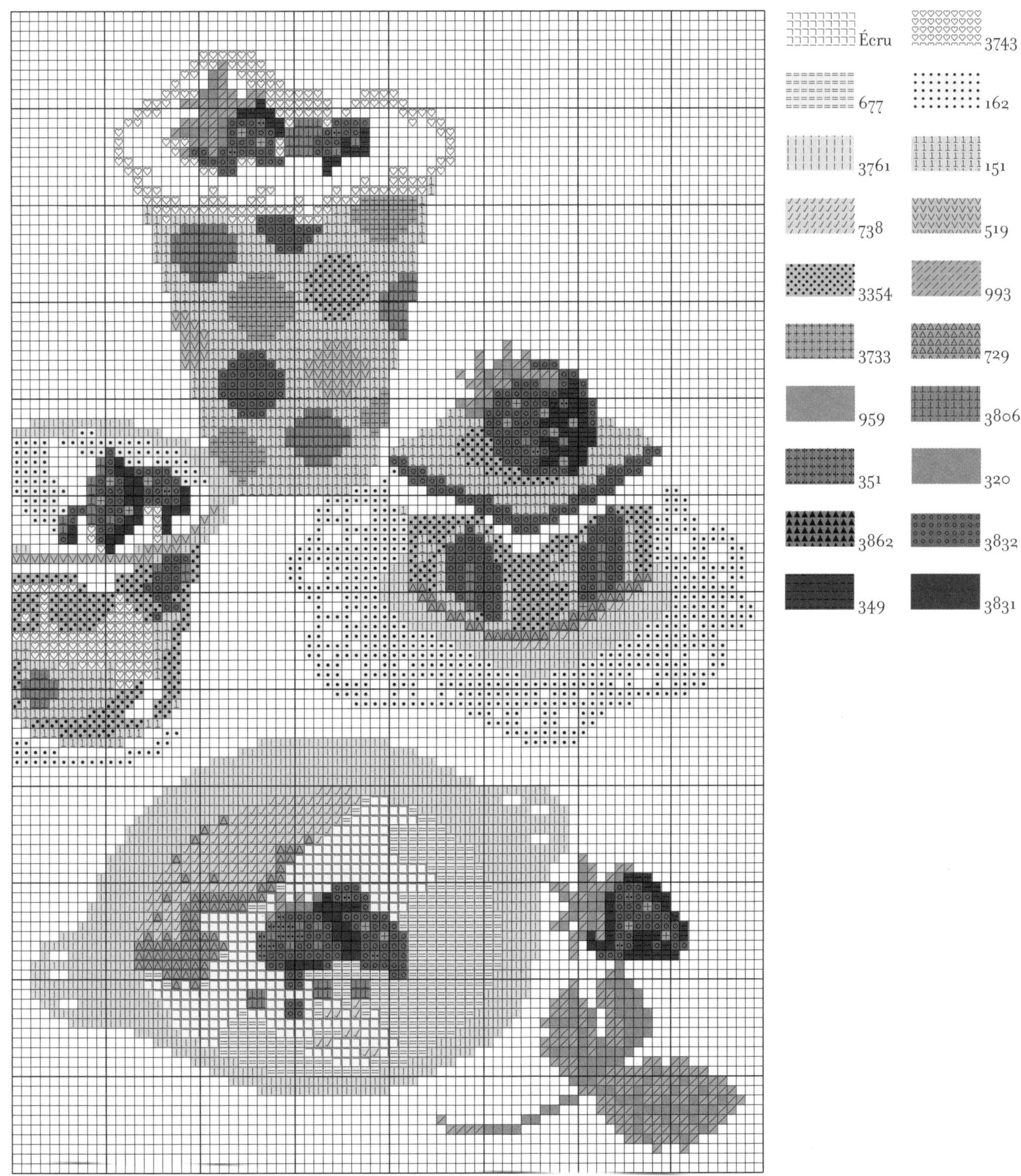
Écru
3743
677
162
3761
151
738
519
3354
993
3733
729
959
3806
351
320
3862
3832
349
3831

Ice-cream desserts / photos pages 34 and 48–49

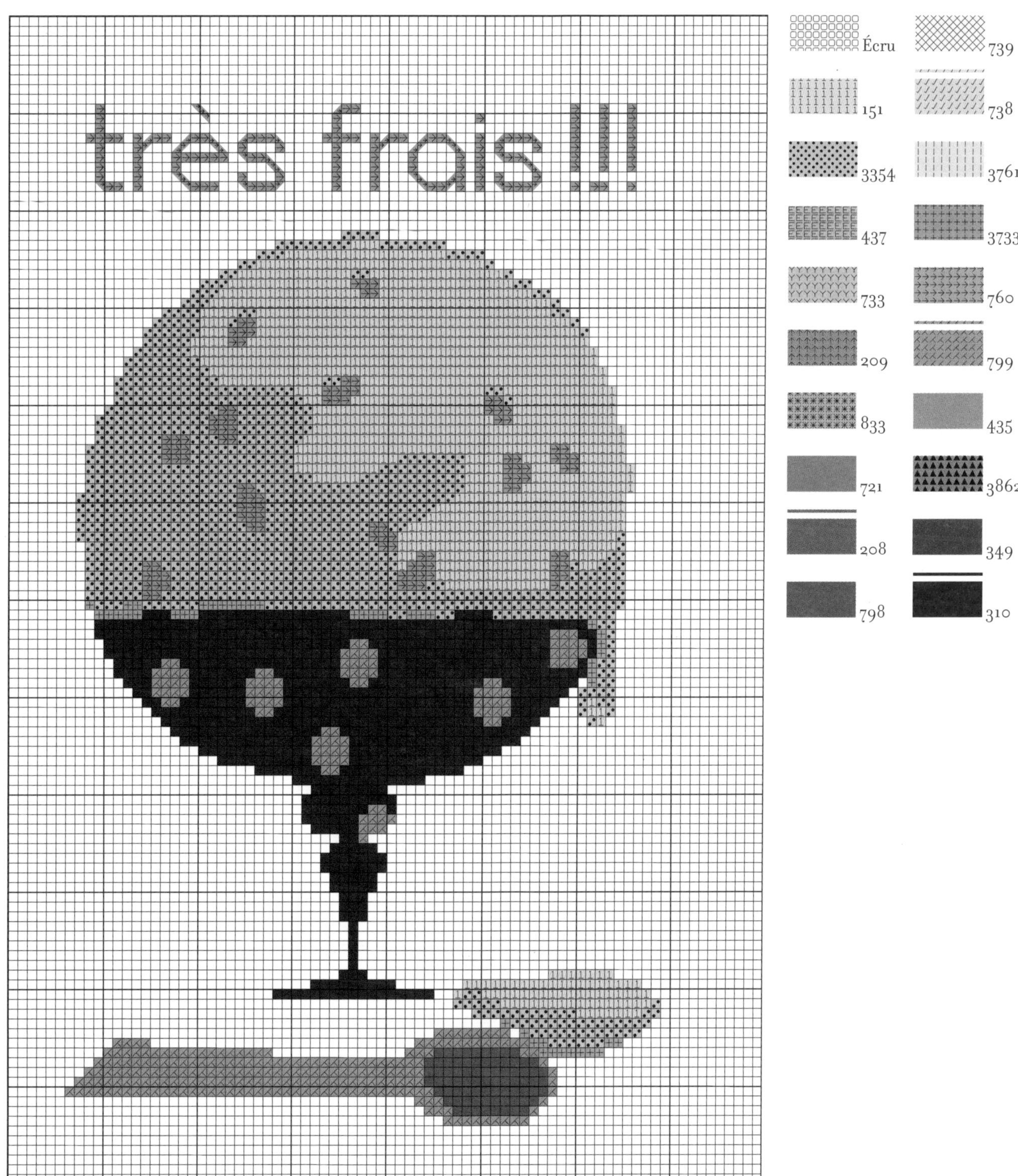

très frais !!!
Écru
739
151
738
3354
3761
437
3733
733
760
209
799
833
435
721
3862
208
349
798
310

'Jours de fête' ('Celebration days') / photos pages 36–37

Jours
de
fête
162
739
437
415
799
318
436
435
3815
349
798
3831
3350
326
310

'C'est Pâques' ('It's Easter') / photos pages 38–39

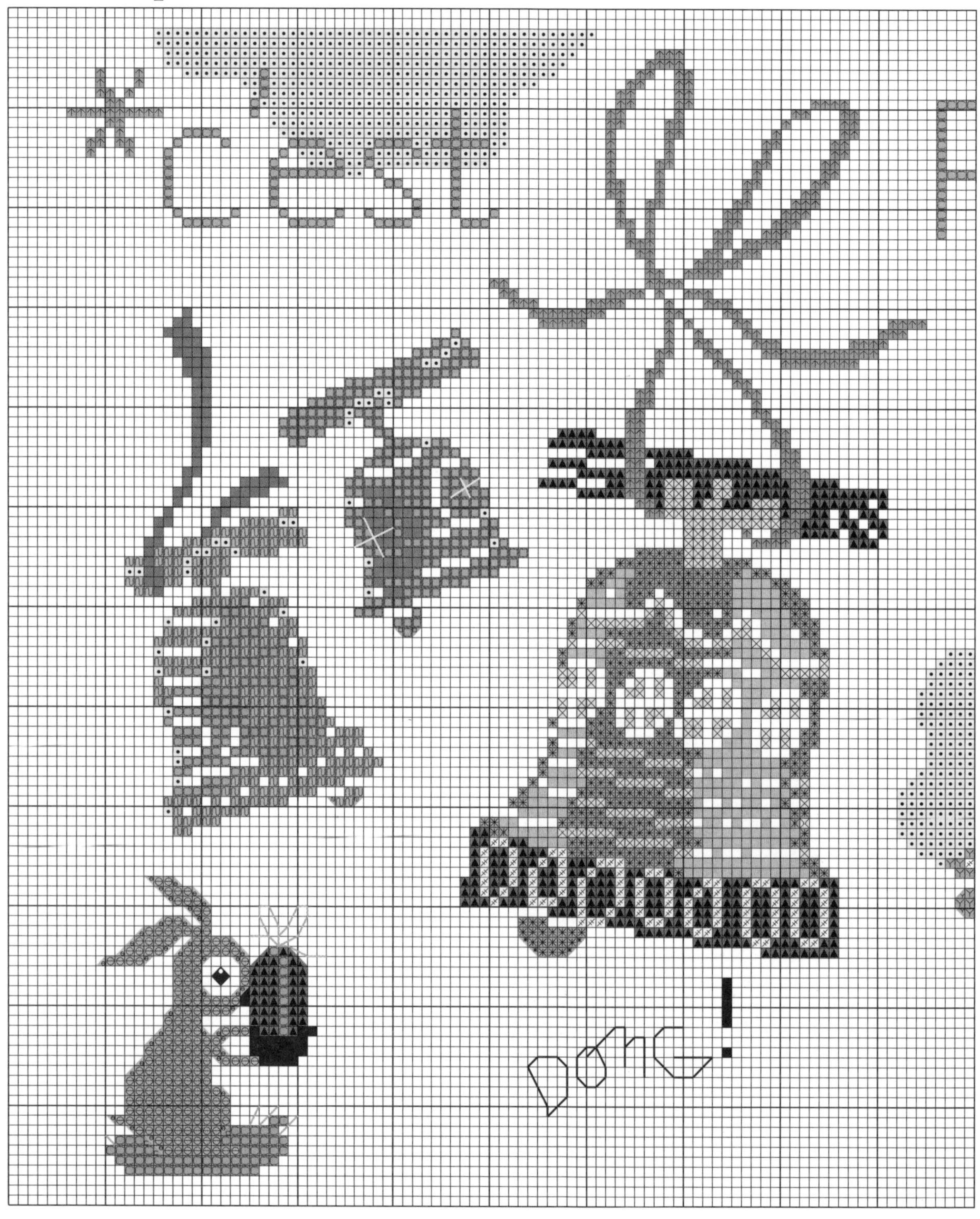

Pâques
822
162
739
3689
834
3755
3045
833
209
597
783
733
160
3862
208
161
310

Afternoon snack / photos pages 40–41

162
644
151
734
519
210
728
761
993
3782
733
760
799
3816
741
3772
351
3839
3862
3832
349
798
898

Pretty alphabets / photos pages 42–43

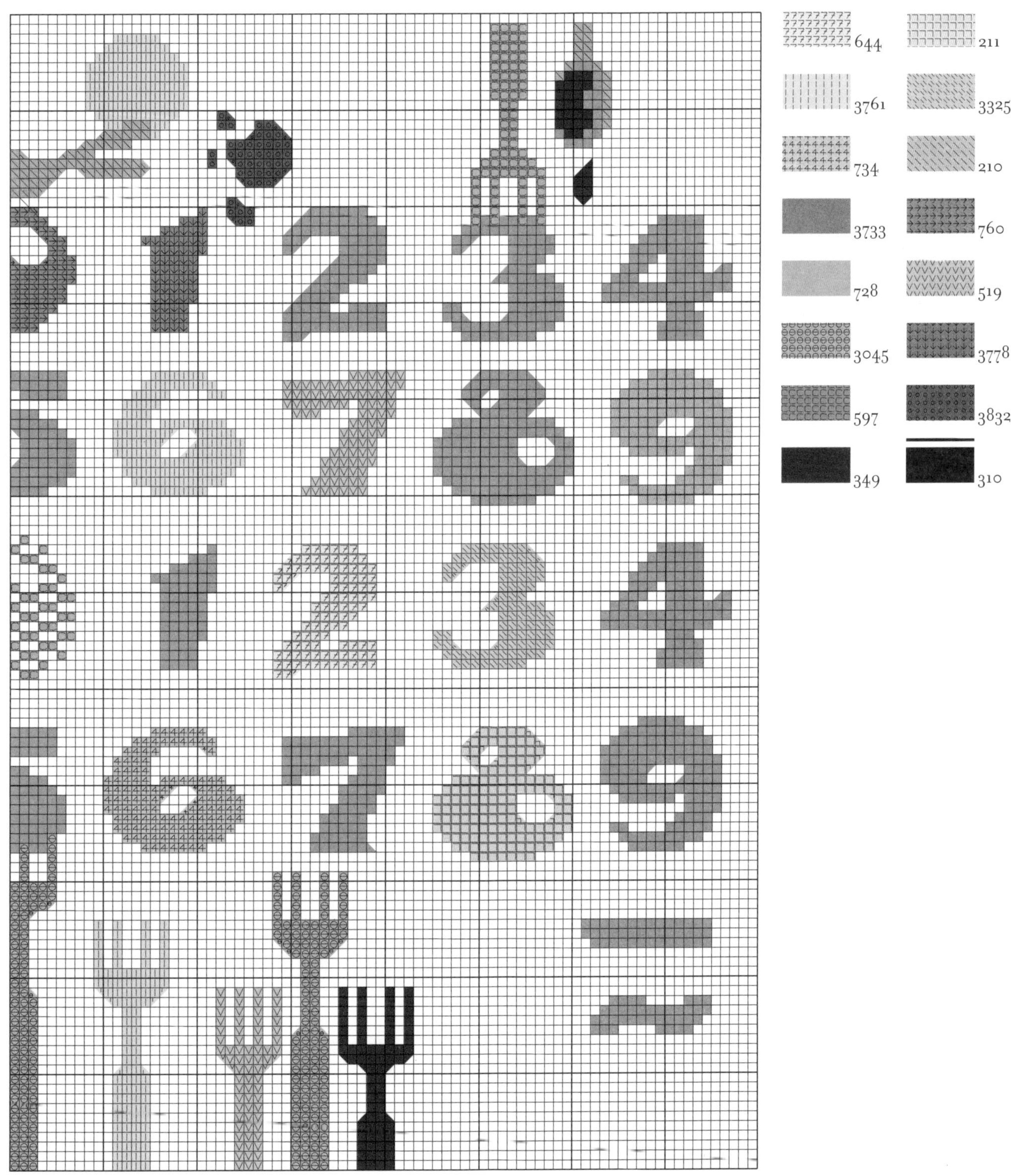
644
211
3761
3325
734
210
3733
760
728
519
3045
3778
597
3832
349
310

Baking tools / photos pages 44–45

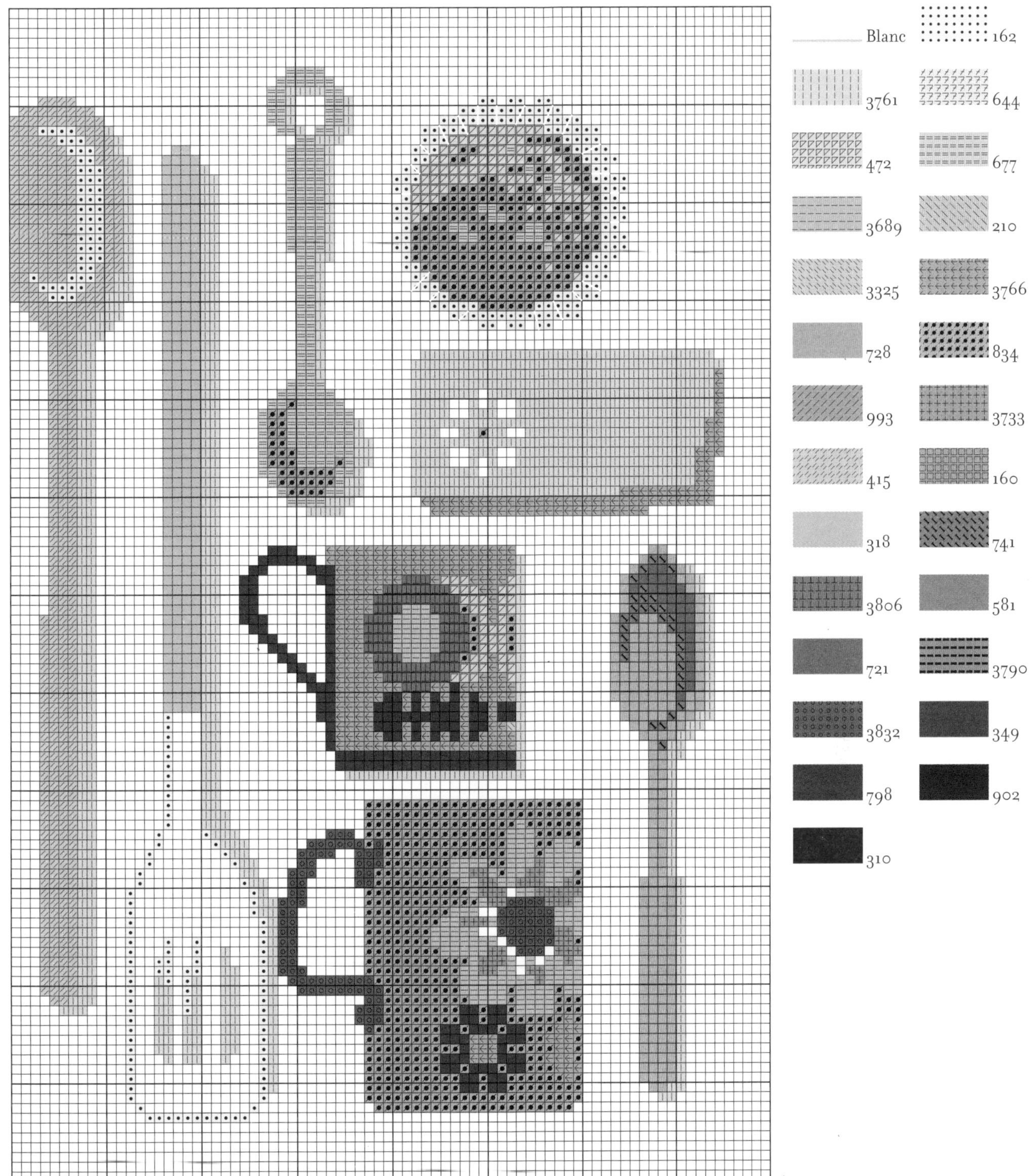
Blanc
162
3761
644
472
677
3689
210
3325
3766
728
834
993
3733
415
160
318
741
3806
581
721
3790
3832
349
798
902
310

Happiness / photos pages 34–5 and 46–47

Blanc
162
728
3761
151
604
993
729
318
959
3806
3832
310

Apple pie / photos pages 50–51

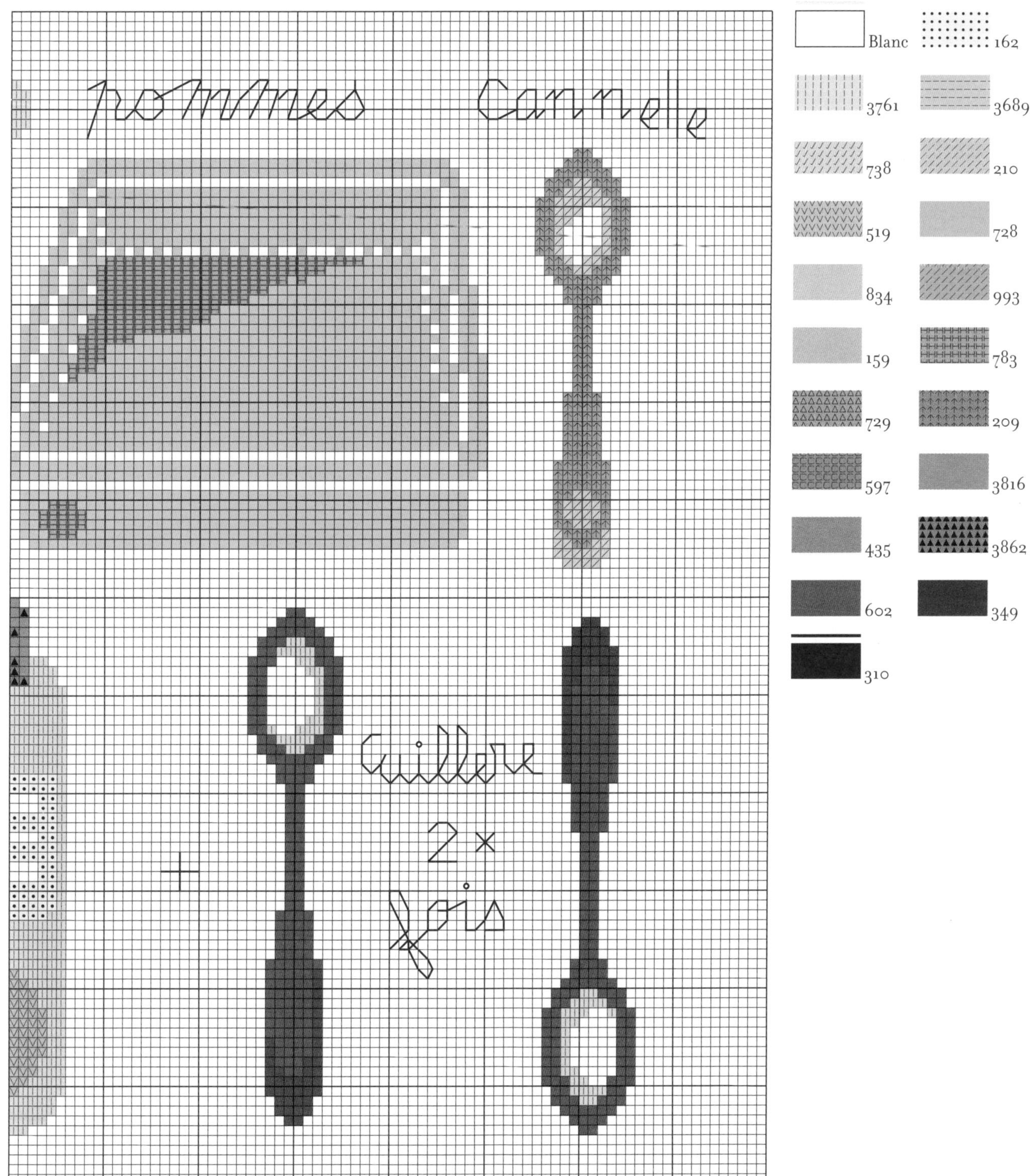
pommes
Cannelle
Cuillere
2 x
fois
Blanc
162
3761
3689
738
210
519
728
834
993
159
783
729
209
597
3816
435
3862
602
349
310

Merry Christmas / photos pages 52–53

Blanc
162
3761
728
519
3733
3045
833
597
3816
3772
435
320
3832
349
310

Sweets and treats / photos pages 54–55 and 59

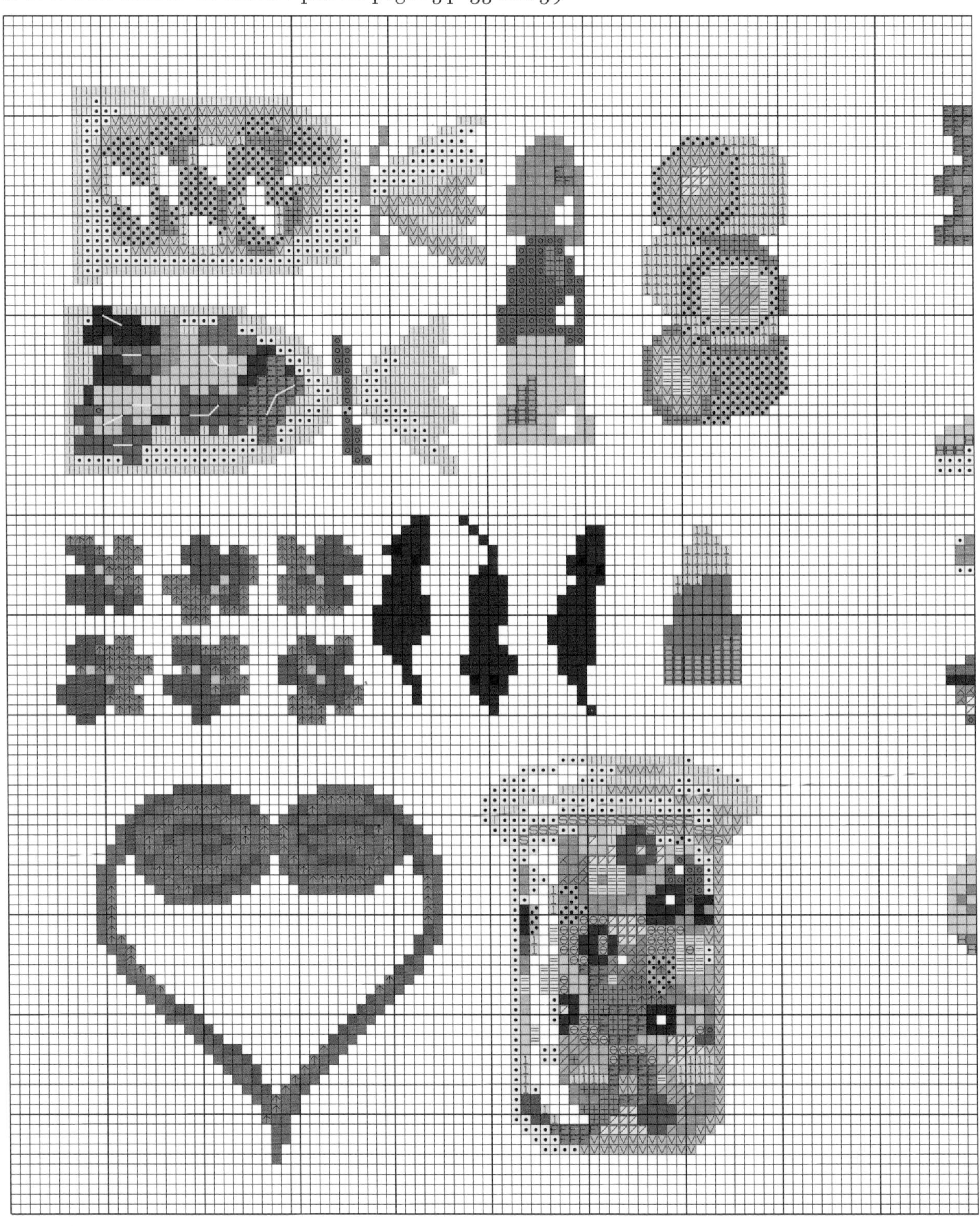

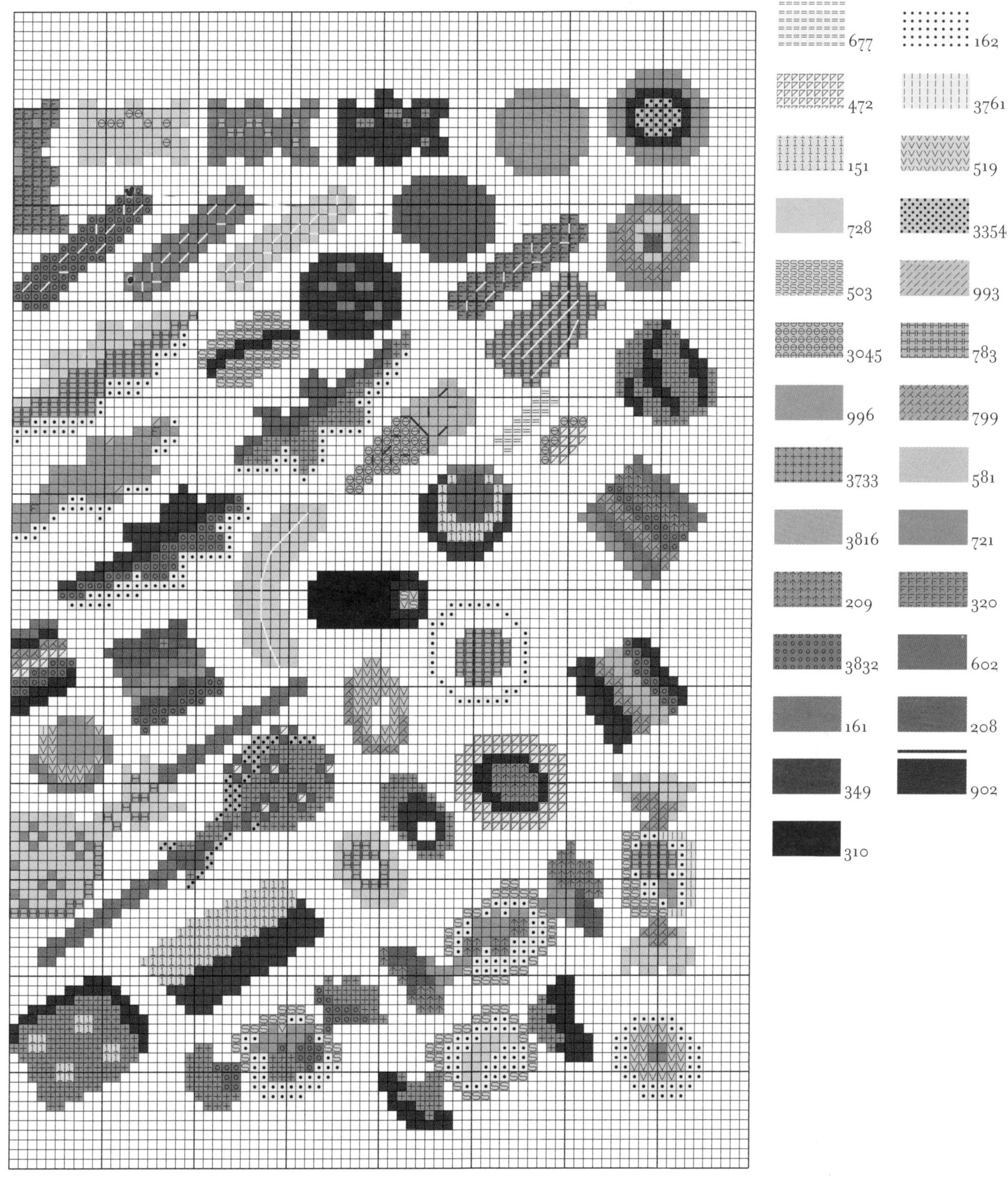
677
162
472
3761
151
519
728
3354
503
993
3045
783
996
799
3733
581
3816
721
209
320
3832
602
161
208
349
902
310

Madeleines / photos pages 33 and 56

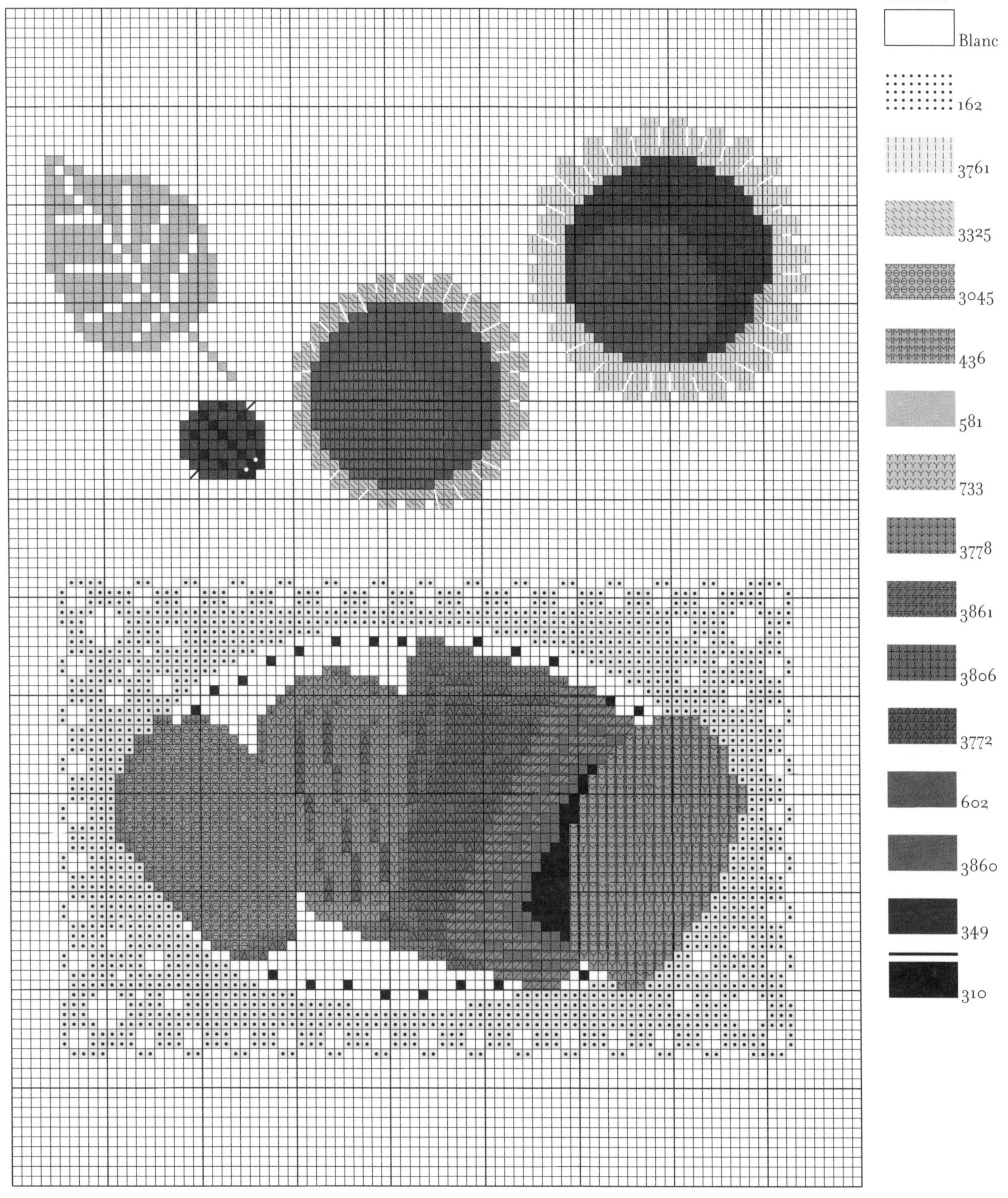

Cookie cutters / photo page 57

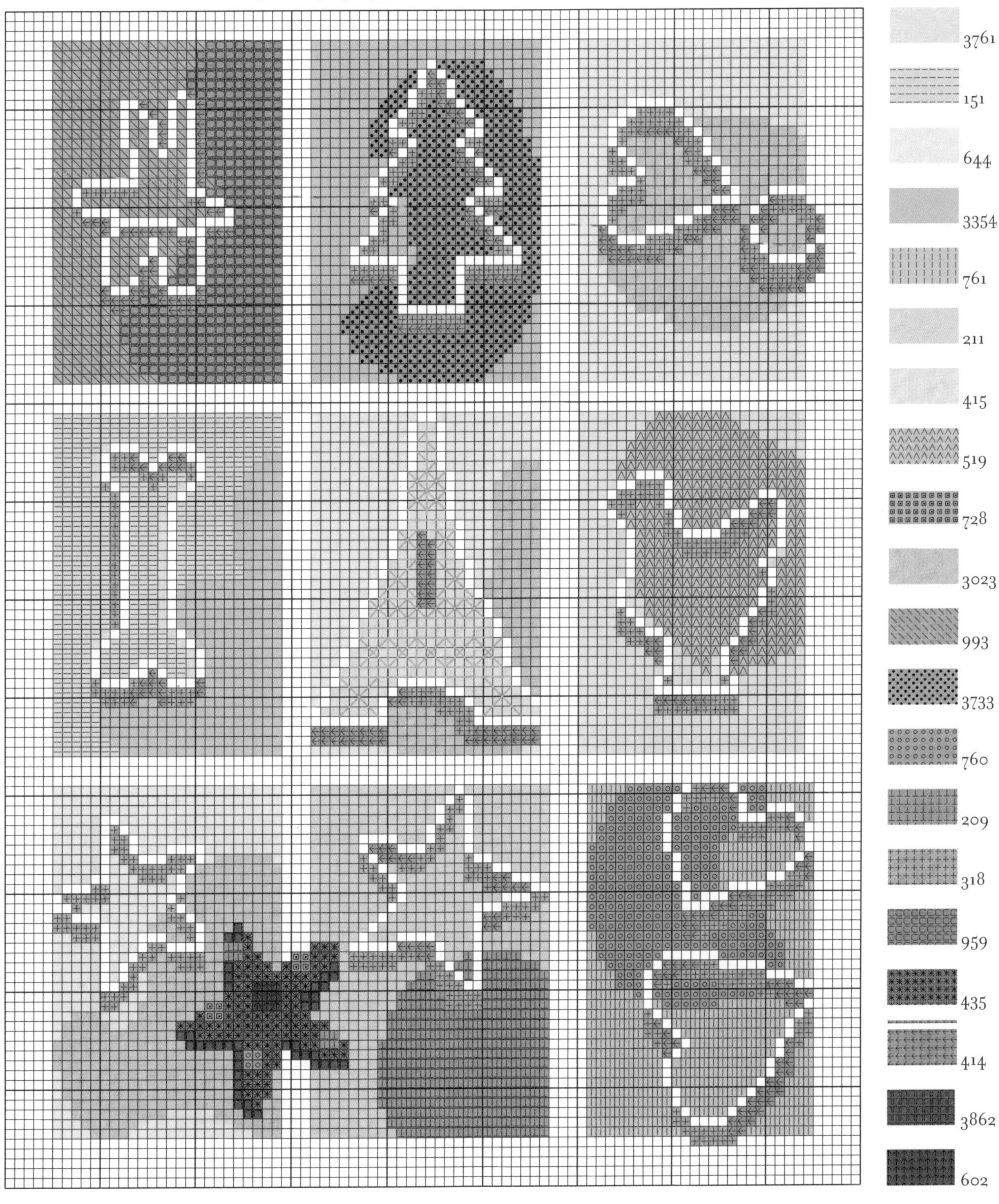

Breakfast à *la française* / photos pages 60–61

Paris
Blanc
162
739
3761
519
728
437
3733
160
783
597
161
435
602
3862
3832
349
798
3831
898
310

C'est chic / photo page 142

'Attention aux moustaches!' ('Watch out for moustaches!') / photo page 29

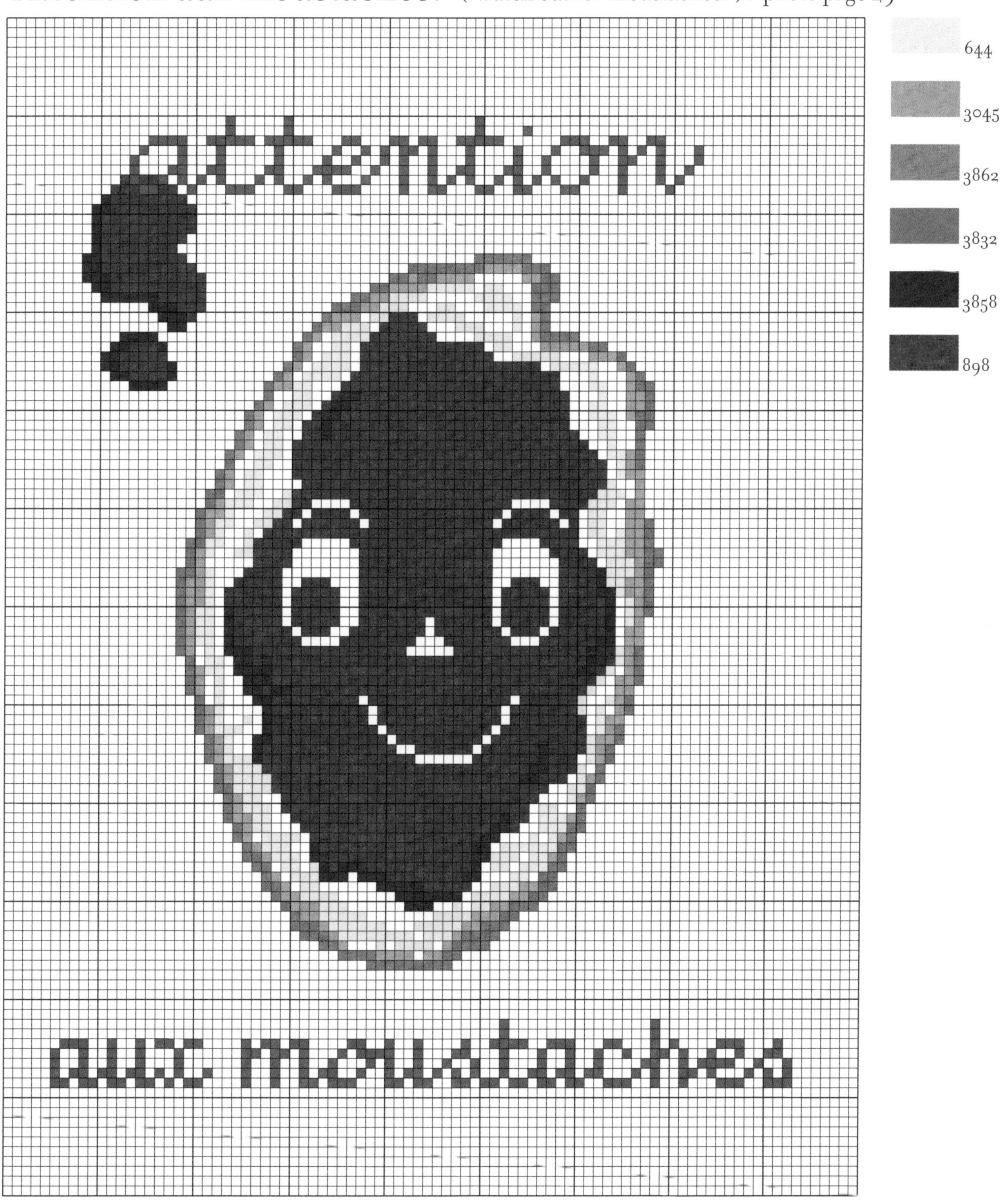

Now for your own tempting treats...

'C'est chic!' wall hanging
instructions page 81
chart page 138

A thought for my friend Nanou, an up-and-coming embroiderer with a sweet tooth!!!

A BIG THANK-YOU...

To Nina, Mona and Ange,
Marino, Lou, Gilles and their lovely house.

First published by Marabout (Hachette Livre) in 2009.

This edition published in 2010 by Murdoch Books Pty Limited

Murdoch Books Australia
Pier 8/9
23 Hickson Road
Millers Point NSW 2000
Phone: +61 (0) 2 8220 2000
Fax: +61 (0) 2 8220 2558
www.murdochbooks.com.au

Murdoch Books UK Limited
Erico House, 6th Floor
93–99 Upper Richmond Road
Putney, London SW15 2TG
Phone: +44 (0) 20 8785 5995
Fax: +44 (0) 20 8785 5985
www.murdochbooks.co.uk

Photography: Frédéric Lucano
Stylist: Sonia Lucano
Design Layout: Frédéric Voisin

Translator: Melissa McMahon
Editor: Sophie Hamley
Project Editor: Laura Wilson
Cover design: Clare O'Loughlin

National Library of Australia Cataloguing-in-Publication entry

Author:	Le Joly Sénoville, Tinou.
Title:	Made in France - sweet treats in cross-stitch : 53 delightful projects to embroider / Tinou Le Joly Sénoville.
ISBN:	978-1-74196-969-6 (pbk.)
Notes:	Includes index.
Subjects:	Cross-stitch Patterns. Desserts in art.
Dewey Number:	746.443041

A catalogue record for this book is available from the British Library.

Printed by 1010 Printing International Limited, China. Reprinted 2011.